BOOKBINDING, AND THE CARE OF BOOKS

WHITE PIGSKIN.—*Basle* 1512

BOOKBINDING, AND THE CARE OF BOOKS

A TEXT-BOOK FOR BOOK-
BINDERS AND LIBRARIANS
BY DOUGLAS COCKERELL WITH
AN APPENDIX
BY SYDNEY M. COCKERELL
DRAWINGS BY NOEL ROOKE
AND OTHER ILLUSTRATIONS

PITMAN · LONDON
TAPLINGER · NEW YORK
A PENTALIC BOOK

PITMAN PUBLISHING LIMITED
39 Parker Street, London WC2B 5PB

Associated Companies
Copp Clark Pitman, Toronto
Pitman Publishing New Zealand Ltd, Wellington
Pitman Publishing Pty Ltd, Melbourne

Published simultaneously in the USA by
Taplinger Publishing Company Inc,
200 Park Avenue South,
New York, N.Y. 10003

First published in Great Britain 1901
Fifth edition 1953
First published in paperback 1978
Reprinted 1979

UK ISBN 0 273 01158 8
US ISBN 0-915798-00-X

Reproduced and printed by photolithography in
Great Britain at The Pitman Press, Bath

EDITOR'S PREFACE

Editor's Preface

In issuing this volume of a series of Handbooks on the Artistic Crafts, it will be well to state what are our general aims.

In the first place, we wish to provide trustworthy text-books of workshop practice, from the points of view of experts who have critically examined the methods current in the shops, and putting aside vain survivals, are prepared to say what is good workmanship, and to set up a standard of quality in the crafts which are more especially associated with design. Secondly, in doing this, we hope to treat design itself as an essential part of good workmanship. During the last century most of the arts, save painting and sculpture of an academic kind, were little considered, and there was a tendency to look on "design" as a mere matter of *appearance*. Such "ornamentation" as there was was usually obtained by following in a mechanical way a drawing provided by an artist who often knew little of the technical process involved in production. With the critical attention given to the crafts by Ruskin and Morris, it came to be seen that it was impossible to detach design from craft in this way, and that, in the widest sense, true design is an inseparable element of good quality, involving as it does the selection of good and suitable material, contrivance for special purpose, expert workmanship, proper finish and so on, far more than mere ornament, and indeed, that ornamentation itself was rather an exuberance of fine workmanship than a matter of merely abstract lines. Workmanship when separated by too wide a gulf from fresh thought—that is from design—inevitably decays, and, on the other hand, ornamentation, divorced from workmanship, is necessarily unreal, and quickly falls into affectation. Proper ornamentation may be defined as a language addressed to the eye; it is pleasant thought expressed in the speech of the tool.

In the third place, we would have this series put artistic craftsmanship before people as furnishing reasonable occupations for those who would gain a livelihood. Although within the bounds of academic art, the competition, of its kind, is so acute that only a very few per cent. can fairly hope to succeed as painters and sculptors; yet, as artistic craftsmen, there is every probability that nearly every one who would pass through a sufficient period of apprenticeship to workmanship and design would reach a measure of success.

In the blending of handwork and thought in such arts as we propose to deal with, happy careers may be found as far removed from the dreary routine of hack labour, as from the terrible uncertainty of academic art. It is desirable in every way that men of good education should be brought back into the productive crafts: there are more than enough of us "in the city," and it is probable that more consideration will be given in this century than in the last to Design and Workmanship.

W. R. LETHABY

AUTHOR'S NOTE

Author's Note

It is hoped that this book will help bookbinders and librarians to select sound methods of binding books.

It is intended to supplement and not to supplant workshop training for bookbinders. No one can become a skilled workman by reading text-books, but to a man who has acquired skill and practical experience, a text-book, giving perhaps different methods from those to which he has been accustomed, may be helpful.

My thanks are due to many friends, including the workmen in my workshop, for useful suggestions and other help, and to the Society of Arts for permission to quote from the report of their Special Committee on Leather for Bookbinding.

I should also like to express my indebtedness to my master, Mr. T. J. Cobden-Sanderson, for it was in his workshop that I learned my craft, and anything that may be of value in this book is due to his influence.

D. C.

A NOTE ON THE FIFTH EDITION

My father wrote this book over seventy five years ago, and in spite of changes that have taken place in that time it is still one of the best books on the subject: besides describing how the operations of binding a book are done, it gives the reasons why books should be bound in certain ways.

I learnt my craft from my father in our workshop at Letchworth, and we found new ways of doing things and developed them. Prior to his death in 1945 it was his intention to revise this book and include some of this new information.

In any living craft, while the basis remains the same, procedure changes from time to time, and some becomes added to the tradition.

I am now including notes in the appendix on a number of the more recent technical developments since the first publication of *Bookbinding, and the Care of Books*.

SYDNEY M. COCKERELL

Letchworth, 1977

LIST OF PLATES

PLATE NO.

(*Between pages* 340 *and* 341)

I. German Fifteenth Century. Pigskin.
II. German Fifteenth Century. Calf.
III. Italian Fifteenth Century. Sheepskin.
IV. Italian Sixteenth Century. Goatskin.
V. Half Niger Morocco, with Sides of English Oak.
VI. Niger Morocco, Onlaid Leaves and Shield.
VII. Green Levant Onlaid with Lighter Green Panel and Red Dots.
VIII. Brown Sealskin Onlaid Flowers
IX. Prayer Book for Archbishop's Throne, Canterbury Cathedral.
X. House of Commons Book of Remembrance.
XI. Incunabula, Aberdeen University.
XII. Lectern Bible for Chichester Cathedral.

CONTENTS

PAGE

EDITOR'S PREFACE v

AUTHOR'S NOTE ix

A NOTE ON THE FIFTH EDITION . . . xi

PART I

BINDING

CHAPTER I

Introduction 17

CHAPTER II

Entering—Books in Sheets—Folding—Collating—Pulling to Pieces—Refolding—Knocking out Joints 33

CHAPTER III

Guarding—Throwing Out—Paring Paper—Soaking off India Proofs—Mounting Very Thin Paper—Splitting Paper—Inlaying—Flattening Vellum . 53

CHAPTER IV

Sizing—Washing—Mending 67

CHAPTER V

PAGE

End Papers—Leather Joints—Pressing . . . 80

CHAPTER VI

Trimming Edges before Sewing—Edge Gilding . 92

CHAPTER VII

Marking up—Sewing—Materials for Sewing . . 98

CHAPTER VIII

Fraying out Slips—Gluing up—Rounding and Backing 114

CHAPTER IX

Cutting and Attaching Boards—Cleaning off Back—Pressing 124

CHAPTER X

Cutting in Boards—Gilding and Colouring Edges . 139

CHAPTER XI

Headbanding 147

CHAPTER XII

Preparing for Covering—Paring Leather—Covering—Mitring Corners—Filling-in Boards . . 152

CHAPTER XIII

PAGE
Library Binding—Binding Very Thin Books—Scrap-books—Binding in Vellum—Books covered with Embroidery 173

CHAPTER XIV

Decoration—Tools—Finishing—Tooling on Vellum—Inlaying on Leather 188

CHAPTER XV

Lettering—Blind Tooling—Heraldic Ornament . 215

CHAPTER XVI

Designing for Gold-tooled Decoration . . . 230

CHAPTER XVII

Pasting down End Papers—Opening Books . . 254

CHAPTER XVIII

Clasps and Ties—Metal on Bindings . . . 259

CHAPTER XIX

Leather 263

CHAPTER XX

Paper—Pastes—Glue 280

PART II

CARE OF BOOKS WHEN BOUND

CHAPTER XXI

PAGE
Injurious Influences to which Books are Subjected . 291

CHAPTER XXII

To Preserve Old Bindings—Re-backing . . . 302

SPECIFICATIONS 307
APPENDIX 313
GLOSSARY 333
REPRODUCTIONS OF BINDINGS 339
BIBLIOGRAPHY 341
INDEX 343

PART I

BINDING

CHAPTER I

INTRODUCTION

Introduction

THE reasons for binding the leaves of a book are to keep them together in their proper order, and to protect them. That bindings can be made, that will adequately protect books, can be seen from the large number of fifteenth and sixteenth century bindings now existing on books still in excellent condition. That bindings are made, that fail to protect books, may be seen by visiting any large library, when it will be found that many bindings have their boards loose and the leather crumbling to dust. Nearly all librarians complain that they have to be continually rebinding books, and this not after four hundred, but after only five or ten years.

It is no exaggeration to say that ninety per cent. of the books bound in leather during the last thirty years will need rebinding during the next thirty. The immense expense involved must be a very serious drag on the usefulness of libraries; and as rebinding is always to some extent damaging to the leaves of a book, it is not only on account of the expense that the necessity for it is to be regretted.

The reasons that have led to the production in modern times of bindings that fail to last for a reasonable time are two-fold. The materials are badly selected or prepared, and the method of binding is faulty. Another factor in the decay of bindings, both old and new, is the bad conditions under which they are often kept.

The object of this text-book is to describe the best methods of bookbinding, and of keeping books when bound, taking into account the present-day conditions. No attempt has been made to describe all possible methods, but only such as appear to have answered best on old books. The methods described are for binding that can be done by hand with the aid of simple appliances. Large editions of books are now bound, or rather cased, at an almost incredible speed by the aid of machinery, but all work that needs personal care and thought on each book, is still done, and probably always will be done, by hand. Elaborate machinery can only be economically employed when very large numbers of books have to be turned out exactly alike.

The ordinary cloth "binding" of the trade is better described as casing. The methods being different, it is convenient to distinguish between casing and binding. In binding, the slips are firmly attached to the boards before covering; in casing, the boards are covered separately, and afterwards glued on to the book. Very great efforts have been made in the decoration of cloth covers, and it is a pity that the methods of construction have not been equally considered. If cloth cases are to be looked upon as a temporary binding, then it seems a pity to waste so much trouble on their decoration; and if they are to be looked upon as permanent binding, it is a pity the construction is not better.

For books of only temporary interest, the usual cloth cases answer well enough; but for books expected to have permanent value, some change is desirable.

Valuable books should either be issued in bindings that are obviously temporary, or else in bindings that are strong enough to be considered permanent. The usual cloth case fails as a temporary binding, because the methods employed result in serious damage to the sections of the book, often unfitting them for rebinding, and it fails as a permanent binding on account of the absence of sound construction.

In a temporary publisher's binding, nothing should be done to the sections of a book that would injure them. Plates should be guarded, the sewing should be on tapes, without splitting the head and tail, or "sawing in" the backs, of the sections; the backs should be glued up square without backing. The case may be attached, as is now usual. For a permanent publisher's binding, something like that recommended for libraries (page 173) is suggested, with either leather or cloth on the back.

At the end of the book four specifications are given (page 307). The first is suggested for binding books of special interest or value, where no restriction as to price is made. A binding under this specification may be decorated to any extent that the nature of the book justifies. The second is for good binding, for books of reference and other heavy books that may have a great deal of wear. All the features of the first that make for the strength of the binding are retained, while those less essential, that only add to the appearance, are omitted. Although the binding under this specification would be much cheaper than that carried out under the first, it would still be too expensive for the majority of books in most libraries; and as it would seem to be impossible further to modify this form of binding, without materially reducing its strength, for cheaper work a somewhat different system is recommended. The third specification is recommended for the binding of the general run of small books in most libraries. The fourth is a modification of this for pamphlets and other books of little value, that need to be kept together tidily for occasional reference.

Thanks, in a great measure, to the work

Intro-
duction

of Mr. Cobden-Sanderson, there is in England the germ of a sound tradition for the best binding. The Report of the Committee appointed by the Society of Arts to investigate the cause of the decay of modern leather bindings, should tend to establish a sound tradition for cheaper work. The third specification at the end of this book is practically the same as that given in their Report, and was arrived at by selection, after many libraries had been examined, and many forms of binding compared.

Up to the end of the eighteenth century the traditional methods of binding books had altered very little during three hundred years. Books were generally sewn round five cords, the ends of all of these laced into the boards, and the leather attached directly to the back. At the end of the eighteenth century it became customary to pare down leather until it was as thin as paper, and soon afterwards the use of hollow backs and false bands became general, and these two things together mark the beginning of the modern degradation of binding, so far as its utility as a protection is concerned.

The Society of Arts Committee report

that the bookbinders must share with the leather manufacturers and librarians the blame for the premature decay of modern bindings, because—

"1. Books are sewn on too few, and too thin cords, and the slips are pared down unduly (for the sake of neatness), and are not in all cases firmly laced into the boards. This renders the attachment of the boards to the book almost entirely dependent on the strength of the leather.

"2. The use of hollow backs throws all the strain of opening and shutting on the joints, and renders the back liable to come right off if the book is much used.

"3. The leather of the back is apt to become torn through the use of insufficiently strong headbands, which are unable to stand the strain of the book being taken from the shelf.

"4. It is a common practice to use far too thin leather; especially to use large thick skins very much pared down for small books.

"5. The leather is often made very wet and stretched a great deal in covering, with the result that on drying it is further strained, almost to breaking point, by

Intro-
duction

contraction, leaving a very small margin of strength to meet the accidents of use."

The history of the general introduction of hollow backs is probably somewhat as follows: Leather was doubtless first chosen for covering the backs of books because of its toughness and flexibility; because, while protecting the back, it would bend when the book was opened and allow the back to "throw up" (see fig. 1, A). When gold tooling became common, and the backs of books were elaborately decorated, it was found that the creasing of the leather injured the brightness of the gold and caused it to crack. To avoid this the binders lined up the back until it was as stiff as a block of wood. The back would then not "throw up" as the book was opened, the leather would not be creased, and the gold would remain uninjured (see fig. 1, B). This was all very well for the gold, but a book so treated does not open fully, and indeed, if the paper is stiff, can hardly be got to open at all. To overcome both difficulties the hollow back was introduced, and as projecting bands would have been in the way, the sewing cord was sunk in saw cuts made across the back of the book.

Introduction

The use of hollow backs was a very ingenious way out of the difficulty, as with them the backs could be made to

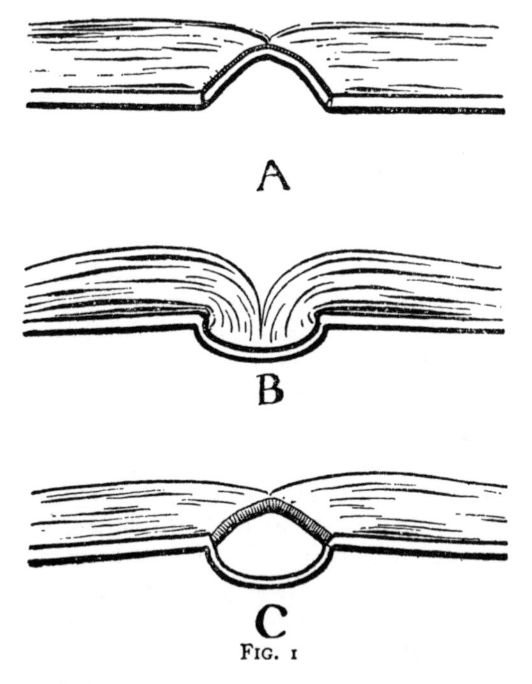

FIG. 1

"throw up," and at the same time the leather was not disturbed (see fig. 1, C). The method of "sawing in" bands was known for a long time before the general use of hollow backs. It has been used to avoid the raised bands on books covered with embroidered material.

If a book is sewn on tapes, and the back lined with leather, there is no serious objection to a carefully-made hollow back without bands. The vellum binders use hollow backs made in this way for great account books that stand an immense amount of wear. They make the "hollow" very stiff, so that it acts as a spring to throw the back up.

But although, if carefully done, satisfactory bindings may be made with hollow backs, their use has resulted in the production of worthless bindings with little strength, and yet with the appearance of better work.

The public having become accustomed to raised bands on the backs of books, and the real bands being sunk in the back, the binders put false ones over the "hollow." To save money or trouble, the bands being out of sight, the books are often sewn on only three or sometimes on only two cords, the usual five false ones still showing at the back. Often only two out of the three bands are laced into the board, and sometimes the slips are not laced in at all.

Again, false headbands worked by the yard by machinery are stuck on at the head and tail, and a "hollow" made with brown paper. Then the book is covered with leather so thin as to have but little strength, and the cover still further weakened by being sprinkled or marbled with injurious iron salts. Books bound in this way cannot last, because the material and construction both lack the element of permanence.

In every large library hundreds of books bound somewhat on these lines may be seen. When they are received from the binder they have the appearance of being well bound, they look smart on the shelf, but in a few years, whether they are used or not, the leather will have perished and the boards become detached, and they will have to be rebound.

As long as librarians expect the appearance of a guinea binding for two or three shillings, such shams will be produced. The librarian generally gets his money's worth, for it would be impossible for the binder to do better work at the price usually paid without materially altering the appearance of the binding. The polished calf and imitation crushed morocco must go, and in its place a rougher, thicker leather must be employed. The full-gilt backs must go, the coloured lettering panel must go, the hollow backs must go, but in the place of these we may have the books sewn on tapes with the ends securely fastened into split boards, and the thick leather attached directly to the backs of the sections. (See specification III, page 309.)

Such a binding would look well and not be more expensive than the usual library binding. It should allow the book to open flat, and if the materials are well selected, be very durable, and specially strong in the joints, the weak place in most bindings. The lettering on the back may be damaged in time if the book is much used, but if so it can easily be renewed at a fraction of the cost of rebinding, and without injury to the book.

While the majority of books in most libraries must be bound at a small cost, at most not exceeding a few shillings a volume, there is a large demand for good plain bindings, and a limited, but growing, demand for more or less decorated bindings for special books.

Any decoration but the simplest should be restricted to books bound as well as the binder can do them. The presence of decoration should be evidence that the binder, after doing his best with the "forwarding," has had time in which to try to make his work a beautiful, as well as a serviceable, production.

Many books, although well bound, are better left plain, or with only a little decoration. But occasionally there are books that the binder can decorate as lavishly as he is able. As an instance of bindings that cannot be over-decorated, those books which are used in important ceremonies, such as Altar Books, may be mentioned. Such books may be decorated with gold and colour until they seem to be covered in a golden material. They will be but spots of gorgeousness in a great church or cathedral, and they cannot be said to be over-decorated as long as the decoration is good.

So, occasionally some one may have a book to which he is for some reason greatly attached, and wishing to enshrine it, give the binder a free hand to do his best with it. The binder may wish to make a delicate pattern with nicely-balanced spots of ornament, leaving the leather for the most part bare, or he may wish to cover the outside with some close gold-tooled pattern, giving a richness of texture hardly to be got by other means. If he decides on the latter, many people will say that the cover is over-decorated. But as a book cover can never be seen absolutely alone, it should not be judged as an isolated thing covered with ornament without relief, but as a spot of brightness and interest among its surroundings. If a room and everything in it is covered with elaborate pattern, then anything with a plain surface would be welcome as a relief; but in a room which is reasonably free from ornament, a spot of rich decoration should be welcome.

It is not contended that the only, or necessarily the best, method of decorating book covers is by elaborate all-over gold-tooled pattern; but it is contended that this is a legitimate method of decoration for exceptional books, and that by its use it is possible to get a beautiful effect well worth the trouble and expense involved.

Good leather has a beautiful surface and may sometimes be got of a fine colour. The binder may often wish to show this surface and colour, and to restrict his decoration to small portions of the cover, and this quite rightly, since he is aiming at, and getting, a totally different effect from that got by all-over patterns. Both methods are right if well done, and both can equally be vulgarised if badly done.

A much debated question is how far the decoration of a binding should be influenced by the contents of the book? A certain appropriateness there should be, but as a general thing, if the binder aims at making the cover beautiful, that is the best he can do. The hints given for designing are not intended to stop the development of the student's own ideas, but only to encourage their development on right lines.

There should be a certain similarity of treatment between the general get-up of a book and its binding. It is a great pity that printers and binders have drifted so far apart; they are, or should be, working for one end, the production of a book, and some unity of aim should be evident in the work of the two.

The binding of manuscripts and early printed books should be strong and simple. It should be as strong and durable as the original old bindings, and, like them, last with reasonable care for four hundred years or more. To this end the old bindings, with their stout sewing cord, wooden boards, and clasps, may be taken as models.

The question is constantly asked, especially by women, if a living can be made by setting up as bookbinders. Cheap binding can most economically be done in large workshops, but probably the best bindings can be done more satisfactorily by binders working alone, or in very small workshops.

If any one intends to set up as a bookbinder, doing all the work without help, it is necessary to charge very high prices to get any adequate return after the working expenses have been paid. In order to get high prices, the standard of work must be very high; and in order to attain a high enough standard of work, a very thorough training is necessary. It is desirable that any one hoping to make money at the craft should have at least a year's training in a workshop where good work is done, and after that, some time will be spent before quite satisfactory work can be turned out rapidly enough to pay, supposing that orders can be obtained or the books bound can be sold.

There are some successful binders who

have had less than a year's training, but they are exceptional. Those who have not been accustomed to manual work have usually, in addition to the necessary skill, to acquire the habit of continuous work. Bookbinding seems to offer an opening for well-educated youths who are willing to serve an apprenticeship in a good shop, and who have some small amount of capital at their command.

Introduction

In addition to the production of decorated bindings, there is much to be done by specialising in certain kinds of work requiring special knowledge. Repairing and binding early printed books and manuscripts, or the restoration of Parish Registers and Accounts, may be suggested.

CHAPTER II

Entering—Books in Sheets—Folding—Collating—Pulling to Pieces—Refolding—Knocking out Joints

ENTERING

Entering

On receiving a book for binding, its title should be entered in a book kept for that purpose, with the date of entry, and

Entering

customer's name and address, and any instructions he may have given, written out in full underneath, leaving room below to enter the time taken on the various operations and cost of the materials used. It is well to number the entry, and to give a corresponding number to the book. It should be at once collated, and any special features noted, such as pages that need washing or mending. If the book should prove to be imperfect, or to have any serious defect, the owner should be communicated with, before it is pulled to pieces. This is very important, as imperfect books that have been "pulled" are not returnable to the bookseller. Should defects only be discovered after the book has been taken to pieces, the bookbinder is liable to be blamed for the loss of any missing leaves.

BOOKS IN SHEETS

Books in Sheets

The sheets of a newly printed book are arranged in piles in the printer's warehouse, each pile being made up of repetitions of the same sheet or "signature." Plates or maps are in piles by themselves.

Books in Sheets

To make a complete book one sheet is gathered from each pile, beginning at the last sheet and working backwards to signature A. When a book is ordered from a publisher in sheets, it is such a "gathered" copy that the binder receives. Some books are printed "double," that is, the type is set up twice, two copies are printed at once at different ends of a sheet of paper, and the sheets have to be divided down the middle before the copies can be separated. Sometimes the title and introduction, or perhaps only the last sheet, will be printed in this way. Publishers usually decline to supply in sheets fewer than two copies of such double-printed books.

If a book is received unfolded, it is generally advisable at once to fold up the sheets and put them in their proper order, with half-title, title, introduction, &c., and, if there are plates, to compare them with the printed list.

Should there be in a recently published book defects of any kind, such as soiled sheets, the publisher will usually replace them on application, although they sometimes take a long time to do so. Such sheets are called "imperfections," and the printers usually keep a number of "overs"

Books in Sheets

in order to make good such imperfections as may occur.

FOLDING

Folding

Books received in sheets must be folded. Folding requires care, or the margins of different leaves will be unequal, and the lines of printing not at right angles to the back.

Books of various sizes are known as "folio," "quarto," "octavo," "duodecimo," &c. These names signify the number of folds, and consequently the number of leaves the paper has been folded into. Thus, a folio is made up of sheets of paper folded once down the centre, forming two leaves and four pages. The sheets of a quarto have a second fold, making four leaves and eight pages, and in an octavo the sheet has a third fold, forming eight leaves and sixteen pages (see fig. 2), and so on. Each sheet of paper when folded constitutes a section, except in the case of folios, where it is usual to make up the sections by inserting two or more sheets, one within the other.

Paper is made in several named sizes, such as "imperial," "royal," "demy,"

Folding

"crown," "foolscap," &c. (see p. 283), so that the terms "imperial folio" or "crown octavo" imply that a sheet of a definite size has been folded a definite number of times.

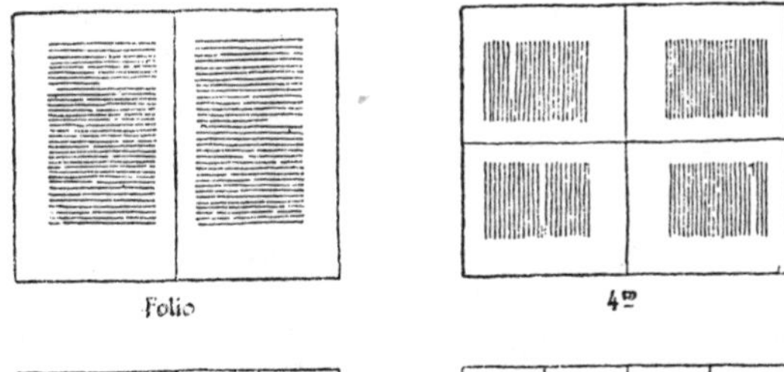

Fig. 2

Besides the traditional sizes, paper is now made of almost any length and width, resulting in books of odd shape, and the names folio, quarto, &c., are rather losing their true meaning, and are often used loosely to signify pages of certain sizes, irrespective of the number that go to a sheet.

Folding

On receipt, for instance, of an octavo book for folding, the pile of sheets is laid flat on the table, and collated by the letter or signature of each sheet. The first sheet of the book proper will probably be signature B, as signature A usually consists of the half-title, title, introduction, &c., and often has to be folded up rather differently.

The "outer" sides, known by the signature letters B, C, D, &c., should be downwards, and the inner sides facing upwards with the second signatures, if there are any, B2, C2, D2, &c., at the right-hand bottom corner.

The pages of an octavo book, commencing at page 1, are shown at fig. 3. A folder is taken in the right hand, and held at the bottom of the sheet at about the centre, and the sheet taken by the left hand at the top right-hand corner and bent over until pages 3 and 6 come exactly over pages 2 and 7; and when it is seen that the headlines and figures exactly match, the paper, while being held in that position, is creased down the centre with the folder, and the fold cut up a little more than half-way. Pages 4, 13, 5, 12 will now be uppermost; pages 12 and 5 are now folded over exactly to match pages 13 and 4, and

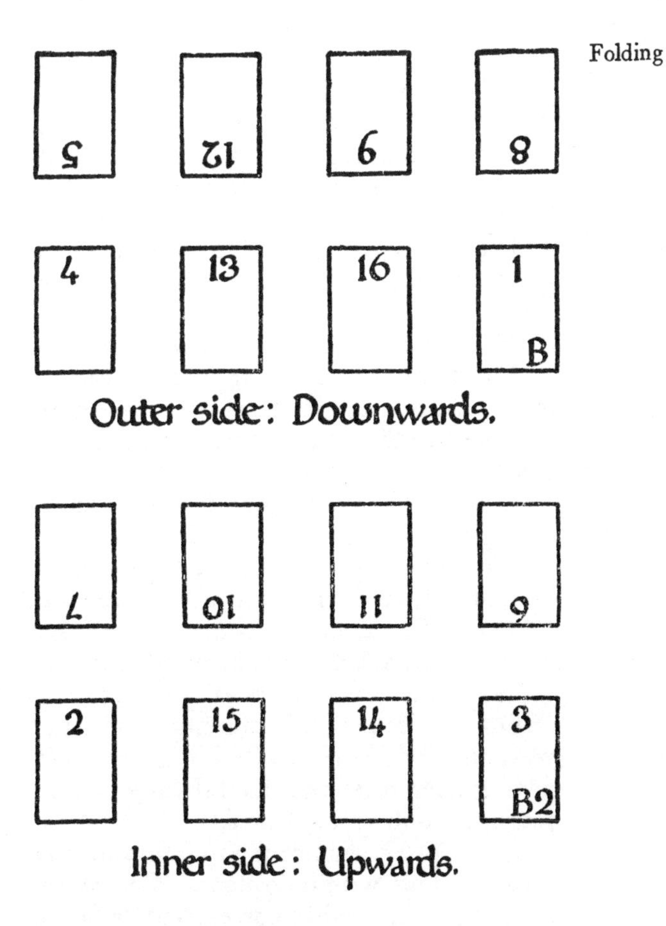

AN OCTAVO SHEET.

FIG. 3

the fold creased and cut up a little more than half-way, as before. Pages 8 and 9 will now be uppermost, and will merely require folding together to make the pages of the section follow in their proper order. If the folding has been done carefully, and the "register" of the printing is good, the headlines should be exactly even throughout.

The object of cutting past the centre at each fold is to avoid the unsightly creasing that results from folding two or more thicknesses of paper when joined at the top edge.

A "duodecimo" sheet has the pages arranged as at fig. 4.

The "inset" pages, 10, 15, 14, 11, must be cut off, and the rest of the section folded as for an octavo sheet. The inset is folded separately and inserted into the centre of the octavo portion.

Other sizes are folded in much the same way, and the principle of folding one sheet having been mastered, no difficulty will be found in folding any other.

Plates often require trimming, and this must be done with judgment. The plates should be trimmed to correspond as far as possible with the printing on the opposite

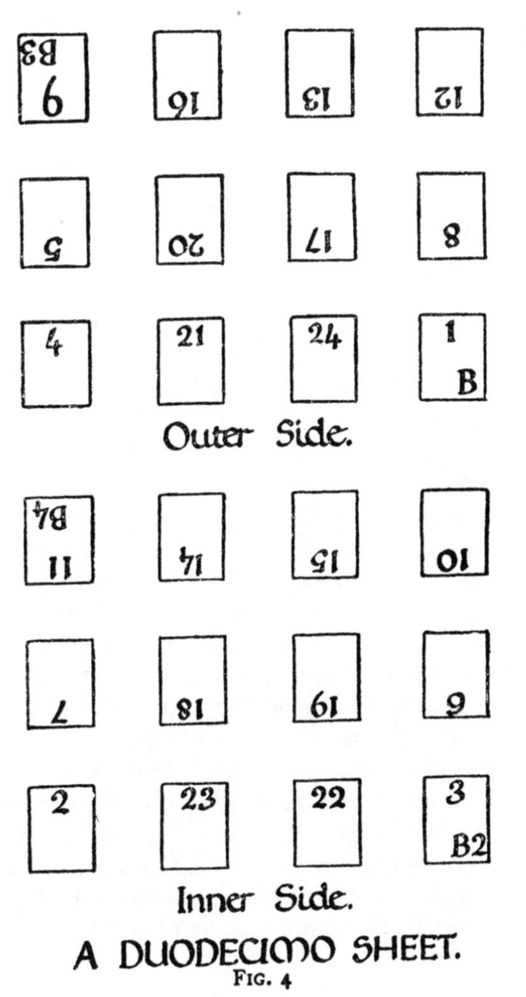

A DUODECIMO SHEET.

Fig. 4

page, but if this cannot be done, it is desirable that something approaching the proportion of margin shown at fig. 2 (folio) should be aimed at. That is to say, the back margin should be the smallest, the head margin the next, the fore-edge a little wider, and the tail widest of all. When a plate consists of a small portrait or diagram in the centre of the page, it looks better if it is put a little higher and a little nearer the back than the actual centre.

Plates that have no numbers on them must be put in order by the list of printed plates, or "instructions to the binder." The half-title, title, dedication, &c., will often be found to be printed on odd sheets that have to be made up into section A. This preliminary matter is usually placed in the following order: Half-title, title, dedication, preface, contents, list of illustrations or other lists. If there is an index, it should be put at the end of the book.

All plates should be "guarded," and any "quarter sections," that is, sections consisting of two leaves, should have their backs strengthened by a "guard," or they may very easily be torn in the sewing. Odd, single leaves may be guarded round sections in the same way as plates.

When a book has been folded, it should be pressed (see p. 87).

Folding

There will sometimes be pages marked by the printer with a star. These have some error in them, and are intended to be cut out. The printer should supply corrected pages to replace them.

COLLATING

Collating

In addition to the pagination each sheet or section of a printed book is lettered or numbered. Each letter or number is called the "sheet's signature." Printers usually leave out J, W and V in lettering sheets. If there are more sections than there are letters in the alphabet, the printer doubles the letters, signing the sections AA, BB, and so on, after the single letters are exhausted. Some printers use an Arabic numeral before the section number to denote the second alphabet, as 2A, 2B, &c., and others change the character of the letters, perhaps using capitals for the first alphabet and italics for the second. If the sheets are numbered, the numbers will of course follow consecutively. In books of more than one volume, the number of the volume is sometimes added in

Roman numerals before the signature, as II A, II B.

The main pagination of the book usually commences with Chapter I, and all before that is independently paged in Roman numerals. It is unusual to have actual numbers on the title or half-title, but if the pages are counted back from where the first numeral occurs, they should come right.

There will sometimes be one or more blank leaves completing sections at the beginning or end. Such blank leaves must be retained, as without them the volume would be "imperfect."

To collate a modern book the paging must be examined to see that the leaves are in order, and that nothing is defective or missing.

The method of doing this is to insert the first finger of the right hand at the bottom of about the fiftieth page, crook the finger, and turn up the corners of the pages with it. When this is done the thumb is placed on page 1, and the hand twisted, so as to fan out the top of the pages. They can then be readily turned over by the thumb and first finger of the left hand (see fig. 5). This is repeated throughout the book, taking about fifty pages at a time. It will of course only be necessary to check the odd numbers, as if they are right, the

Collating

Fig. 5

even ones on the other side of the leaf must be so. If the pages are numbered at the foot, the leaves must be fanned out from the head.

Plates or maps that are not paged can only be checked from the printed list. When checked it will save time if the

Collating

number of the page which each faces is marked on the back in small pencil figures.

In the case of early printed books or manuscripts, which are often not paged, special knowledge is needed for their collation. It may roughly be said, that if the sections are all complete, that is, if there are the same number of leaves at each side of the sewing in all the sections, the book may be taken to be perfect, unless of course whole sections are missing. All unpaged books should be paged through in pencil before they are taken apart; this is best done with a very fine pencil, at the bottom left-hand corner; it will only be necessary to number the front of each leaf.

PULLING TO PIECES

Pulling to Pieces

After the volume has been collated it must be "pulled," that is to say, the sections must be separated, and all plates or maps detached.

If in a bound book there are slips laced in the front cover, they must be cut and the back torn off. It will sometimes happen that in tearing off the leather nearly all the glue will come too, leaving

Pulling to Pieces

the backs of the pages detached except for the sewing. More usually the back will be left covered with a mass of glue and linen, or paper, which it is very difficult to remove without injury to the backs of the sections. By drawing a sharp knife along the bands, the sewing may be cut and the bands removed, leaving the sections only connected by the glue. Then the sections of the book can usually be separated with a fine folder, after the thread from the centre of each has been removed; the point of division being ascertained by finding the first signature of each section. In cases where the glue and leather form too hard a back to yield to this method, it is advisable to soak the glue with paste, and when soft to scrape it off with a folder. As this method is apt to injure the backs of the sections, it should not be resorted to unless necessary; and when it is, care must be taken not to let the damp penetrate into the book, or it will cause very ugly stains. The book must be pulled while damp, or else the glue will dry up harder than before. The separated sections must be piled up carefully to prevent pages being soiled by the damp glue.

Pulling to Pieces

All plates or single leaves "pasted on" must be removed. These can usually be detached by carefully tearing apart, but if too securely pasted they must be soaked off in water, unless of course the plates have been painted with water-colour. If the plates must be soaked off, the leaf and attached plate should be put into a pan of slightly warm water and left to soak until they float apart, then with a soft brush any remaining glue or paste can be easily removed while in the water. Care must be taken not to soak modern books printed on what is called "Art Paper," as this paper will hardly stand ordinary handling, and is absolutely ruined if wetted. The growing use of this paper in important books is one of the greatest troubles the bookbinder has to face. The highly loaded and glazed surface of some of the heavy plate papers easily flakes off, so that any guard pasted on these plates is apt to come away, taking with it the surface of the paper. Moreover, should the plates chance to be fingered or in any way soiled, nothing can remove the marks; and should a corner get turned down, the paper breaks and the corner will fall off. It is the opinion of experts that this heavily loaded Art Paper will not last a reasonable time, and, apart from other considerations, this should be ample reason for not using it in books that are expected to have a permanent value. Printers like this paper, because it enables them to obtain brilliant impressions from blocks produced by cheap processes.

Pulling to Pieces

In "cased" books, sewn by machinery, the head and tail of the sheets will often be found to be split up as far as the "kettle" stitches. If such a book is to be expensively bound, it will require mending throughout in these places, or the glue may soak into the torn ends and make the book open stiffly.

Some books are put together with staples of tinned iron wire, which rapidly rust and disfigure the book by circular brown marks. Such marks will usually have to be cut out and the places carefully mended. This process is lengthy, and consequently so costly that it is generally cheaper, when possible, to obtain an unbound copy of the book from the publishers, than to waste time repairing the damage done by the cloth binder.

Generally speaking, the sections of a book cased in cloth by modern methods are so injured as to make it unfit for more permanent binding unless an unreasonable amount of time is spent on it. It is a great pity that publishers do not, in the case of books expected to have a permanent literary value, issue a certain number of copies printed on good paper, and unbound, for the use of those who require permanent bindings; and in such copies it would be a great help if sufficient margin were left at the back of the plates for the binder to turn it up to form a guard. If the plates were very numerous, guards made of the substance of the plates themselves would make the back too thick; but in the case of books with not more than a dozen plates, printed on comparatively thin paper, this plan is satisfactory.

Some books in which there are a large number of plates are cut into single leaves, which are held together at the back by a coating of an indiarubber solution. For a short time such a volume is pleasant enough to handle, and opens freely, but before long the indiarubber perishes, and the leaves and plates fall apart. When a book of this kind comes to have a permanent binding, all the leaves and plates have to be pared at the back and made up into sections with guards—a troublesome and expensive business. The custom with binders is to overcast the backs of the leaves in sections, and to sew through the overcasting thread, but this, though an easy and quick process, makes a hopelessly stiff back, and no book so treated can open freely.

Pulling to Pieces

REFOLDING

Refolding

When the sheets of books that have to be rebound have been carelessly folded, a certain amount of re-adjustment is often advisable, especially in cases where the book has not been previously cut. The title-page and the half-title, when found to be out of square, should nearly always be put straight. The folding of the whole book may be corrected by taking each pair of leaves and holding them up to the light and adjusting the fold so that the print on one leaf comes exactly over the print on the

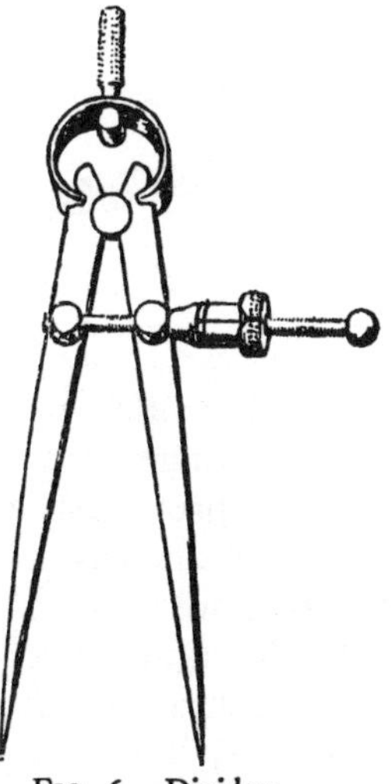

FIG. 6.—Dividers

Refolding

other, and creasing the fold to make them stay in that position. With a pair of dividers (fig. 6) set to the height of the shortest top margin, points the same distance above the headline of the other leaves can be made. Then against a carpenter's

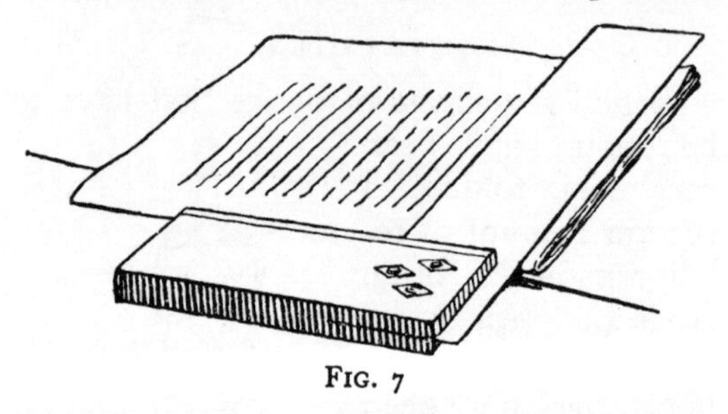

FIG. 7

square, adjusted to the back of the fold, the head of one pair of leaves at a time can be cut square (see fig. 7). If the book has been previously cut this process is apt to throw the leaves so far out of their original position as to make them unduly uneven.

Accurate folding is impossible if the "register" of the printing is bad, that is to say, if the print on the back of a leaf does not lie exactly over that on the front.

Crooked plates should usually be made straight by judicious trimming of the margins. It is better to leave a plate short at tail or fore-edge than to leave it out of square.

Refolding

KNOCKING OUT JOINTS

Knocking out Joints

The old "joints" must be knocked out of the sections of books that have been previously backed. To do this, one or two sections at a time are held firmly in the left hand, and well hammered on the knocking-down iron fixed into the lying press. It is important that the hammer face should fall exactly squarely upon the paper, or it may cut pieces out. The knocking-down iron should be covered with a piece of paper, and the hammer face must be perfectly clean, or the sheets may be soiled.

CHAPTER III

Guarding—Throwing Out—Paring Paper—Soaking off India Proofs—Mounting Very Thin Paper—Splitting Paper—Inlaying—Flattening Vellum

GUARDING

Guarding

GUARDS are slips of thin paper or linen used for strengthening the fold of leaves that are damaged, or for attaching plates or single leaves.

Guards should be of good thin paper. That known as Whatman's Banknote paper

Guarding

answers very well. An easy way to cut guards is shown in fig. 8. Two or three pieces of paper of the height of the required guards are folded and pinned to the board by the right-hand corners. A series of points are marked at the head and tail with dividers set to the width desired for the guards, and with a knife guided by a straight-edge, cuts joining the points are made right through the paper, but not extending quite to either end. On a transverse cut being made near the bottom, the guards are left attached by one end only (see fig. 9), and can be torn off as wanted. This method prevents the paper from slipping while it is being cut.

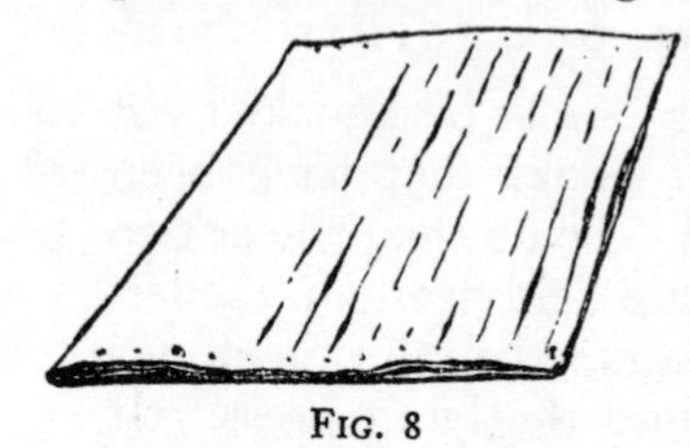

FIG. 8

FIG. 9

A mount cutter's knife (fig. 10) will be found to be a convenient form of knife to use for cutting guards.

Guarding

In using the knife and straight-edge a good deal of pressure should be put on the straight-edge, and comparatively little on the knife.

To mend the torn back of a pair of leaves, a guard should be selected a little

FIG. 10.—Mount Cutter's Knife

longer than the height of the pages and well pasted with white paste (see page 288). If the pair of leaves are not quite separated, the pasted guard held by its extremities may be simply laid along the weak place and rubbed down through blotting-paper. If the leaves are quite apart, it is better to lay the pasted guard on a piece of glass and put the edges of first one and then the other leaf on to it and rub down.

On an outside pair of leaves the guard should be inside, so that the glue may catch any ragged edges; while on the inside pair the guard should be outside, or it will be found to be troublesome in sewing. In handling the pasted guards care is needed not to stretch them, or they may cause the sheet to crinkle as they dry.

Guarding

Plates must be guarded round the sections next them. Where there are a great many plates the back margin of each, to which a guard will be attached, must be pared (see fig. 11, A), or the additional thickness caused by the guards

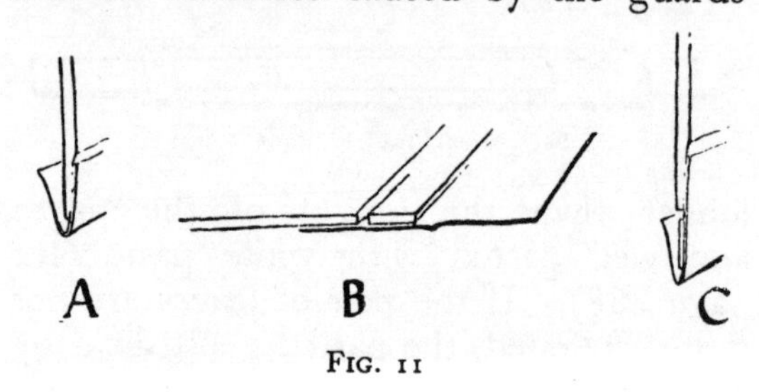

FIG. 11

will make the back swell unduly. In guarding plates a number can be pasted at once if they are laid one on another, with about an eighth of an inch of the back of each exposed, the top of the pile being protected by a folded piece of waste paper (see fig. 12). To paste, the brush is brought from the top to the bottom of the pile only, and not the other way, or paste will get between the plates and soil them. Guards should usually be attached to the backs of plates, and should be wide enough to turn up round the adjoining section, so that they may be sewn through. Should a plate come in the middle of a section, the guard is best turned back and slightly pasted to the inside of the sheet and then sewn through in the ordinary way.

Guarding

If plates are very thick, they must be

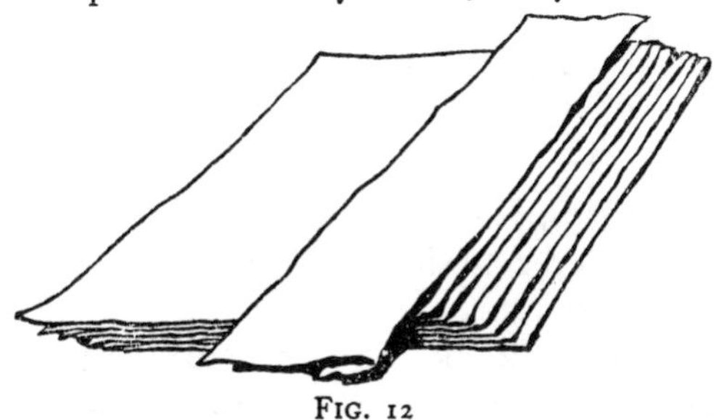

FIG. 12

hinged, as shown at fig. 11, B. This is done by cutting a strip of about a quarter of an inch off the back of the plate, and guarding with a wide guard of linen, leaving a small space between the plate and the piece cut off to form a hinge. It will save some swelling if the plate is pared and a piece of thinner paper substituted for the piece cut off (see fig. 11, C). If the plates are of cardboard, they should be guarded on both sides with linen, and may even need a second joint.

A book that consists entirely of plates

Guarding

or single leaves must be made up into sections with guards, and sewn as usual. In books in which there are a great many plates, it is often found that two plates either come together in the centre of a section, or come at opposite sides of the

FIG. 13

same pair of leaves. Such plates should be guarded together and treated as folded sheets (see fig. 13).

In order to be sure that the pages of a book to be guarded throughout will come in their proper order, it is well to make a plan of the sections as follows, and to check each pair of leaves by it, as they are guarded—

Thus, if the book is to be made up into sections of eight leaves, the pairs of leaves to be guarded together can be seen at once if the numbers of the pages are written out—

1, 3, 5, 7,—9, 11, 13, 15.

First the inside pair, 7 and 9, are guarded together with the guard outside, then the next pair, 5 and 11, then 3 and 13, and then the outside pair, 1 and 15, which should have the guard inside. A plan for the whole book would be more conveniently written thus—

Guarding

1–15	17–31	33–47
3–13	19–29	35–45
5–11	21–27	37–43
7–9	23–25	39–41, and so on.

To arrange a book of single leaves for guarding, it is convenient to take as many leaves as you intend to go to a section, and opening them in the centre, take a pair at a time as they come.

The number of leaves it is advisable to put into a section will depend on the thickness of the paper and the thickness and size of the book. If the paper is thick, and the backs of the leaves have been pared, four leaves to a section will be found to answer. But if the paper is thin, and does not allow of much paring, it is better to have a larger section, in order to have as little thread in the back as possible.

The sheets of any guarded book should be pressed before sewing, in order to reduce the swelling of the back caused by the guards.

Throwing Out

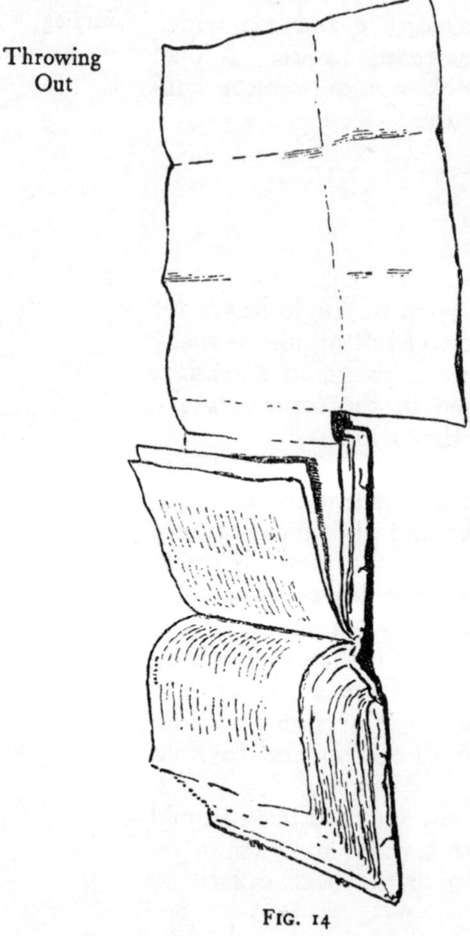
FIG. 14

THROWING OUT

Maps or diagrams that are frequently referred to in the text of a book, should be "thrown out" on a guard as wide as the sheet of the book. Such maps, &c., should be placed at the end, so that they may lie open for reference (see fig. 14). Large folded maps or diagrams should be mounted on linen. To do this take a piece of jaconet and after damping it slightly pin it out flat on the board, then evenly paste the back of the map with thin paste in which there are no lumps, and lay it on the linen, rub down through blotting-paper, and leave to dry. Unless the pasting is done evenly the marks of the paste-brush will

Throwing Out

FIG. 15

show through the linen. If a folded map is printed on very thick paper each fold must be cut up, and the separate pieces mounted on the linen, with a slight space between them to form a flexible joint.

A folded map must have in the back of the book sufficient guards to equal it in thickness at its thickest part when folded, or the book will not shut properly (see fig. 15).

PARING PAPER

Paring Paper

For paring the edge of paper for mending or guarding, take a very sharp knife,

Paring Paper

and holding the blade at right angles to the covering-board, draw the edge once or twice along it from left to right. This should turn up enough of the edge to form a "burr," which causes the knife to cut while being held almost flat on the paper. The plate or paper should be laid face downwards on the glass with the edge to be pared away from the workman, the knife held in the right hand, with the burr downwards. The angle at which to hold the knife will depend on its shape and on the thickness and character of the paper to be pared, and can only be learned by practice. If the knife is in order, and is held at the proper angle, the shaving removed from a straight edge of paper should come off in a long spiral. If the knife is not in proper order, the paper may be badly jagged or creased.

SOAKING OFF INDIA PROOFS

Soaking off India Proofs

Place a piece of well-sized paper in a pan of warm water, then lay the mounted India proof, face downwards, upon it and leave it to soak until the proof floats off. Then carefully take out the old mount, and the India proof can be readily removed from the water on the under paper, and dried between sheets of blotting-paper.

Soaking off India Proofs

MOUNTING VERY THIN PAPER

Very thin paper, such as that of some "India" proofs, may be safely mounted as follows:—The mount, ready for use, is laid on a pad of blotting-paper. The thin paper to be mounted is laid face downwards on a piece of glass and very carefully pasted with thin, white paste. Any paste on the glass beyond the edges of the paper is carefully wiped off with a clean cloth. The glass may then be turned over, and the pasted plate laid on the mount, its exact position being seen through the glass.

Mounting Very Thin Paper

SPLITTING PAPER

It is sometimes desirable to split pieces of paper when the matter on one side only is needed, or when the matter printed on each side is to be used in different places. The paper to be split should be well pasted on both sides with a thickish paste, and fine linen or jaconet placed on each side. It is then nipped in the press to

Splitting Paper

Splitting Paper

make the linen stick all over, and left to dry.

If the two pieces of jaconet are carefully pulled apart when dry, half the paper should be attached to each, unless at any point the paste has failed to stick, when the paper will tear. The jaconet and paper attached must be put into warm water until the split paper floats off.

INLAYING LEAVES OR PLATES

Inlaying Leaves or Plates

When a small plate or leaf has to be inserted into a larger book, it is best to "inlay it"; that is to say, the plate or leaf is let into a sheet of paper the size of the page of the book. To do this, a piece of paper as thick as the plate to be inlaid, or a little thicker, is selected, and on this is laid the plate, which should have been previously squared, and the positions of the corners marked with a folder. A point is made about an eighth of an inch inside each corner mark, and the paper within these points is cut out (see fig. 16). This leaves a frame of paper, the

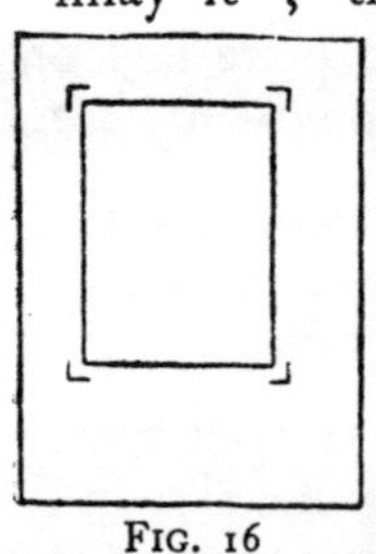

Fig. 16

inner edges of which will slightly overlap the edges of the plate. The under edge of the plate, and the upper edge of the mount, should then be pared and pasted, and the plate laid in its place (with the corners corresponding to the folder marks). If the edges have been properly pared, the thickness where they overlap should not exceed the thickness of the frame paper. If an irregular fragment is to be inlaid, it is done in the same way, except that the entire outline is traced on the new paper with a folder, and the paper cut away, allowing one eighth of an inch inside the indented line.

Inlaying Leaves or Plates

FLATTENING VELLUM

Flattening Vellum

The leaves of a vellum book that have become cockled from damp or other causes may be flattened by damping them, pulling them out straight, and allowing them to dry under pressure. To do this take the book to pieces, clean out any dirt there may be in the folds of the leaves, and spread out each pair of leaves as flatly as possible.

Damp some white blotting-paper by interleaving it with common white paper

Flattening Vellum

that has been wetted with a sponge. One sheet of wet paper to two of blotting-paper will be enough. The pile of blotting-paper and wet paper is put in the press and left for an hour or two under pressure, then taken out and the common paper removed.

The blotting-paper should now be slightly and evenly damp. To flatten the vellum the open pairs of leaves are interleaved with the slightly damp blotting-paper, and are left for an hour under the weight of a pressing-board. After this time the vellum will have become quite soft, and can with care be flattened out and lightly pressed between the blotting-paper, and left for a night. The next day the vellum leaves should be looked at to see that they lie quite flat, and the blotting-paper changed for some that is dry. The vellum must remain under pressure until it is quite dry, or it will cockle up worse than ever when exposed to the air. The blotting-paper should be changed every day or two. The length of time that vellum leaves take to dry will vary with the state of the atmosphere, and the thickness of the vellum, from one to six weeks.

Almost any manuscript or printed book on vellum can be successfully flattened in this way; miniatures should have pieces of waxed paper laid over them to prevent the chance of any of the fibres of the blotting-paper sticking. The pressure must not be great; only enough is needed to keep the vellum flat as it dries.

Flattening Vellum

This process of flattening, although so simple, requires the utmost care. If the blotting-paper is used too damp, a manuscript may be ruined; and if not damp enough, the pressing will have no effect.

CHAPTER IV

Sizing—Washing—Mending

SIZING

THE paper in old books is sometimes soft and woolly. This is generally because the size has perished, and such paper can often be made perfectly sound by re-sizing.

Sizing

For size, an ounce of isinglass or good gelatine is dissolved in a quart of water. This should make a clear solution when

Sizing

gently warmed, and should be used at about a temperature of 120° F. Care must be taken not to heat too quickly, or the solution may burn and turn brown. If the size is not quite clear, it should be strained through fine muslin or linen

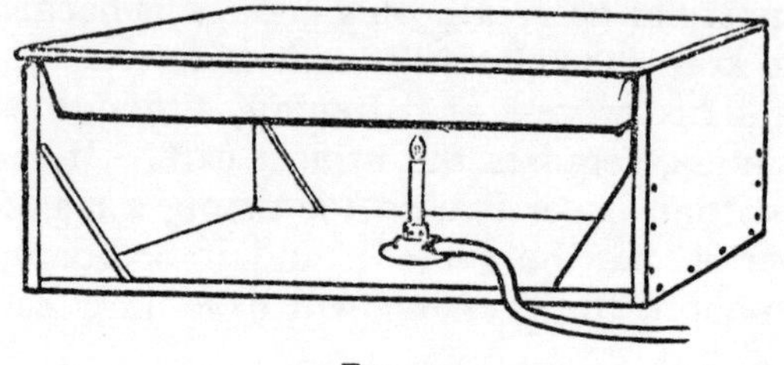

FIG. 17

before being used. When it is ready it should be poured into an open pan (fig. 17), so arranged that it can be kept warm by a gas flame or spirit lamp underneath. When this is ready the sheets to be sized can be put in one after another and taken out at once. The hot size will be found to take out a great many stains, and especially those deep brown stains that come from water. If there are only a few sheets, they can be placed between blotting paper as they are removed from the size; but if there is a whole book, it is best to lay them in a pile one on the other and when all have been sized to squeeze them in the "lying press" between pressing-boards, a pan being put underneath to catch the liquid squeezed out. When the sheets have been squeezed they can be readily handled, and should be spread out to dry on a table upon clean paper. When they are getting dry and firm they can be hung on strings stretched across the room, slightly overlapping one another. The strings must first be covered with slips of clean paper, and the sized sheets should have more paper over them to keep them clean.

Sizing

Before sizing it will be necessary to go through a book and take out any pencil or dust marks that can be removed with indiarubber or bread crumbs, or the size will fix them, and it will be found exceedingly difficult to remove them afterwards.

When the sheets are dry they should be carefully mended in any places that may be torn, and folded up into sections and pressed. A long, comparatively light pressure will be found to flatten them better and with less injury to the surface of the paper than a short, very heavy pressure, such as that of the rolling-machine.

In some cases it will be found that

sheets of old books are so far damaged as to be hardly strong enough to handle. Such sheets must be sized in rather a stronger size in the following way:—Take a sheet of heavily-sized paper, such as notepaper, and carefully lay your damaged sheet on that. Then put another sheet of strong paper on the top, and put all three sheets into the size. It will be found that the top sheet can then be easily lifted off, and the size be made to flow over the face of the damaged sheet. Then, if the top sheet be put on again, the three sheets, if handled as one, can be turned over and the operation repeated, and size induced to cover the back of the damaged leaf. The three sheets must then be taken out and laid between blotting-paper to take up the surplus moisture. The top sheet must then be carefully peeled off, and the damaged page laid face downwards on clean blotting-paper. Then the back sheet can be peeled off as well, leaving the damaged sheet to dry.

The following is quoted from *Chambers's Encyclopædia* on Gelatine—

"Gelatine should never be judged by the eye alone.

"Its purity may be very easily tested thus: Soak it in cold water, then pour upon it a small quantity of boiling water. If pure, it will form a thickish, clear straw-coloured solution, free from smell; but if made of impure materials, it will give off a very offensive odour, and have a yellow gluey consistency."

Sizing

WASHING

Washing

When there are stains or ink marks on books that cannot be removed by the use of hot size or hot water, stronger measures may sometimes have to be taken. Many stains will be found to yield readily to hot water with a little alum in it, and others can be got out by a judicious application of curd soap with a very soft brush and plenty of warm water. But some, and especially ink stains, require further treatment. There are many ways of washing paper, and most of those in common use are extremely dangerous, and have in many cases resulted in the absolute destruction of fine books. If it is thought to be absolutely necessary that the sheets of a book should be washed, the safest method is as follows:—Take an ounce of permanganate of potash dissolved

Washing

in a quart of water, and warmed slightly. In this put the sheets to be washed, and leave them until they turn a dark brown. This will usually take about an hour, but may take longer for some papers. Then turn the sheets out and wash them in running water until all trace of purple stain disappears from the water as it comes away. Then transfer them to a bath of sulphurous (not sulphuric) acid and water in the proportion of one ounce of acid to one pint of water. The sheets in this solution will rapidly turn white, and if left for some time nearly all stains will be removed. In case any stains refuse to come out, the sheets should be put in clear water for a short time, and then placed in the permanganate of potash solution again, and left there for a longer time than before; then after washing in clear water, again transferred to the sulphurous acid. When sheets are removed from the sulphurous acid they should be well washed for an hour or two in running water, and then may be blotted or squeezed off and hung up on lines to dry. Any sheets treated in this way will require sizing afterwards. And if, as is often the case, only a few sheets at the beginning or end of the book have to be washed, it will be necessary to tone down the washed sheets to match the rest of the book by putting some stain in the size. For staining there are many things used. A weak solution of permanganate of potash gives a yellowish stain that will be found to match many papers. Other stains are used, such as coffee, chicory, tea, liquorice, &c. Whatever is used should be put in the size. To ascertain that the right depth of colour has been obtained, a piece of unsized paper, such as white blotting-paper, is dipped in the stained size and blotted off and dried before the fire. It is impossible to judge of the depth of colour in a stain unless the test piece is thoroughly dried. If the stain is not right, add more water or more stain as is needed. Experience will tell what stain to use to match the paper of any given book.

To remove grease or oil stains, ether may be used. Pour it freely in a circle round the spot, narrowing the circle gradually until the stain is covered. Then apply a warm iron through a piece of blotting-paper.

Ether should only be used in a draught in a well-ventilated room on account of its well-known inflammable and anæsthetical properties.

A very dilute (about one per cent.) solution of pure hydrochloric acid in cold water will be found to take out some stains if the paper is left in it for some hours. When the paper is removed from the solution, it must be thoroughly washed in running water. It is important that the hydrochloric acid used should be pure, as the commercial quality (spirits of salts) often contains sulphuric acid.

The following recipes are quoted from *De l'organisation et de l'administration des Bibliothèques, par Jules Cousin*—

To remove stains from paper:—"*Mud Stains.*—To take away these kinds of stains, spread some soap jelly very evenly over the stained places, and leave it there for thirty or forty minutes, according to the depth of the stain. Then dip the sheet in clean water, and then having spread it on a perfectly clean table, remove the soap lightly with a hog's hair brush or a fine sponge; all the mud will disappear at the same time. Put the sheet into the clear water again, to get rid of the last trace of soap. Let it drain a little, press it lightly between two sheets of blotting-paper, and finish by letting it dry slowly in a dry place in the shade.

"*Stains of Tallow, Stearine or Fat.*—To take away these stains cover them with blotting-paper and pass over them a warm flat-iron. When the paper has soaked up the grease, change it and repeat the operation until the stains have been sufficiently removed. After that, touch both sides of the sheets where they have been stained with a brush dipped in essence of turpentine heated to boiling-point. Then to restore the whiteness of the paper, touch the places which were stained with a piece of fine linen soaked in purified spirits of wine warmed in the water-bath. This method may also be employed to get rid of sealing-wax stains.

"*Oil Stains.*—Make a mixture of 500 gr. of soap, 300 gr. of clay, 60 gr. of quicklime, and sufficient water to make it of the right consistency, spread a thin layer of this on the stain, and leave it there about a quarter of an hour. Then dip the sheet in a bath of hot water; take it out, and let it dry slowly.

"You can also use the following method generally employed for finger-marks—

"*Finger-marks.* — These stains are

Washing

sometimes very obstinate. Still they can generally be mastered by the following method:—Spread over them a layer of white soap jelly (*savon blanc en gelée*), and leave it there for some hours. Then remove this with a fine sponge dipped in hot water, and more often than not all the dirt disappears at the same time. If this treatment is not sufficient, you might replace the soap jelly by soft soap (*savon noir*), but you must be careful not to leave it long on the printing, which might decompose and run, and that would do more harm than good."

Sheets of very old books are best left with the stains of age upon them, excepting, perhaps, such as can be removed with hot water or size. Nearly all stains *can* be removed, but in the process old paper is apt to lose more in character than it gains in appearance.

MENDING

Mending

For mending torn sheets of an old book, some paper that matches as nearly as possible must be found. For this purpose it is the custom for bookbinders to collect quantities of old paper. If a piece of the same tone cannot be found, paper of similar texture and substance may be stained to match.

Supposing a corner to be missing, and a piece of paper to have been found that matches it, the torn page is laid over the new paper in such a way that the wire marks on both papers correspond. Then the point of a folder should be drawn along the edge of the torn sheet, leaving an indented line on the new paper. The new paper should then be cut off about an eighth of an inch beyond the indented line, and the edge carefully pared up to the line. The edge of the old paper must be similarly pared, so that the two edges when laid together will not exceed the thickness of the rest of the page. It is well to leave a little greater overlap at the edges of the page. Both cut edges must then be well pasted with white paste and rubbed down between blotting-paper. To ensure a perfectly clean joint the pasted edge should not be touched with the hand, and pasting-paper, brushes, and paste must be perfectly clean.

In the case of a tear across the page, if there are many overlapping edges, they may merely be pasted together and the end of the tear at the edge of the paper strengthened by a small piece of pared paper. If the tear crosses print, and there are no overlapping edges, either tiny pieces of pared paper may be cut and laid across the tear between the lines of print, or else a piece of the thinnest Japanese paper, which is nearly transparent, may be pasted right along the tear over the print; in either case the mend should be strengthened at the edge of the page by an additional thickness of paper. In cases where the backs of the sections have been much damaged, it will be necessary to put a guard the entire length, or in the case of small holes, to fill them in with pieces of torn paper. The edges of any mend may, with great care, be scraped with a sharp knife having a slight burr on the under side, and then rubbed lightly with a piece of worn fine sand-paper, or a fragment of cuttle-fish bone. Care must be taken not to pare away too much, and especially not to weaken the mend at the edges of the sheet. As a general rule, the new mending paper should go on the back of a sheet.

Sometimes it is thought necessary to fill up worm-holes in the paper. This may be done by boiling down some paper in size until it is of a pulpy consistency, and a little of this filled into the worm-holes will re-make the paper in those places. It is a very tedious operation, and seldom worth doing.

Mending

Mending vellum is done in much the same way as mending paper, excepting that a little greater overlap must be left. It is well to put a stitch of silk at each end of a vellum patch, as you cannot depend on paste alone holding vellum securely. The overlapping edges must be well roughed up with a knife to make sure that the paste will stick. A cut in a vellum page is best mended with fine silk with a lacing stitch (see fig. 18).

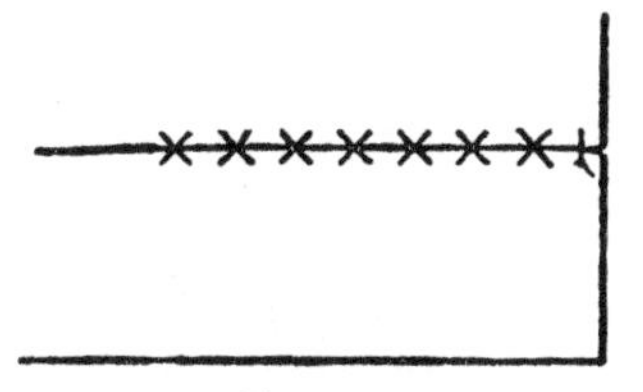

FIG. 18

Mending is most easily done on a sheet of plate-glass, of which the edges and corners have been rubbed down.

CHAPTER V

End Papers—Leather Joints—Pressing

END PAPERS

End Papers

If an old book that has had much wear is examined, it will generally be found that the leaves at the beginning and the end have suffered more than the rest of the book. On this ground, and also to enable people who must write notes in books to do so with the least injury to the book, it is advisable to put a good number of blank papers at each end. As these papers are part of the binding, and have an important protective function to perform, they should be of good quality. At all times difficulty has been found in preventing the first and last sections of the book, whether end papers or not, from dragging away when the cover is opened, and various devices have been tried to overcome this defect. In the fifteenth century strips of vellum (usually cut from manuscripts) were pasted on to the back of the book and on the inside of the boards, or in some cases were merely folded round the first and last sections and pasted on to the covers. The modern, and far less efficient, practice is to "overcast" the first and last sections. This is objectionable, because it prevents the leaves from opening right to the back, and it fails in the object aimed at, by merely transferring the strain to the back of the overcast section.

In order to make provision for any strain there may be in opening the cover, it is better to adopt some such arrangement as shown in fig. 19. In this end paper the zigzag opens slightly in response to any strain.

The way to make this end paper is to take a folded sheet of paper a little larger than the book. Then with dividers mark two points an eighth of an inch from the back for the fold, and paste your paste-down paper, BB, up to these points (see fig. 19, II). When the paste is dry, fold back the sheet (A1) over the paste-down paper, and A2 the reverse way, leaving the form seen in fig. 19, III. A folded sheet of paper similar to A is inserted at C (fig. 19, V, H), and the sewing passes through this. When the

End Papers

book is pasted down the leaf A1 is torn off, and B1 pasted down on the board. If marbled paper is desired, the marble

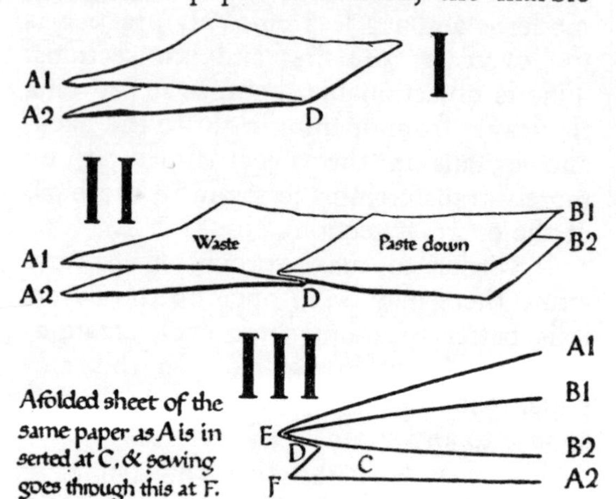

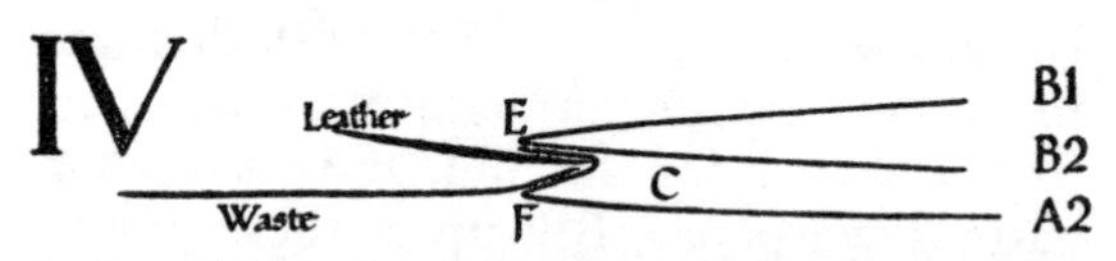

Leather and Waste are folded over B1 at E and a folded sheet inserted at C. Sewing goes through both E and F.

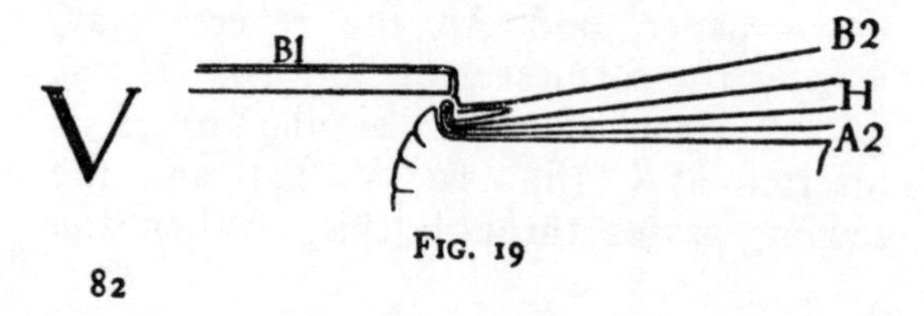

FIG. 19

should be "made," that is, pasted on to B1.

End Papers

There are considerable disadvantages in using marbled papers, as if they are of thick enough paper to help the strength of the binding, the "made" sheet is very stiff, and in a small book is troublesome. On no account should any marbled paper be used unless it is tough and durable. The quality of the paper of which most marbled papers are made is so poor that it is unsuitable for use as end papers. For most books a self-coloured paper of good quality answers well for the paste-down sheets.

It is a mistake to leave end papers to be pasted on after the book has been forwarded, as in that case they have little constructive value. Every leaf of such an end paper as is described above will open right to the back, and the zigzag allows play for the drag of the board.

Paper with a conventional pattern painted or printed on it may be used for end papers. If such a design is simple, such as a sprig repeated all over, or an arrangement of stars or dots, it may look very well; but over elaborate end papers, and especially those that aim at pictorial effect, are seldom successful.

Ends may be made of thin vellum. If so, unless the board is very heavy, it is best to have leather joints.

A single leaf of vellum (in the place of B1 and 2, II, fig. 19) should have an edge turned up into the zigzag with the leather joint, and sewn through. Vellum ends must always be sewn, as it is not safe to rely upon paste to hold them. They look well, and may be enriched by tooling. The disadvantage of vellum is that it has a tendency to curl up if subjected to heat, and when it contracts it unduly draws the boards of the book. For large manuscripts, or printed books on vellum, which are bound in wooden or other thick boards and are clasped, thicker vellum may be used for the ends; that with a slightly brown surface looks best. The part that will come into the joint should be scraped thin with a knife, and a zigzag made of Japanese paper.

Silk or other fine woven material may be used for ends. It is best used with a leather joint, and may be stuck on to the first paper of the end papers (B1, II, fig. 19), and cut with the book. The glaire of the edge gilding will help to stop the edges fraying out. In attaching silk to paper, thin glue is the best thing to use; the paper, not the silk, being glued. Some little practice is needed to get sufficient glue on the paper to make the silk stick all over, and yet not to soil it. When the silk has been glued to the paper, it should be left under a light weight to dry. If put in the press, the glue may be squeezed through and the silk soiled.

If the silk is very thin, or delicate in colour, or if it seems likely that it will fray out at the edges, it is better to turn the edges in over a piece of paper cut a little smaller than the page of the book and stick them down. This forms a pad, which may be attached to the first leaf of the end papers; a similar pad may be made for filling in the board.

Before using, the silk should be damped and ironed flat on the wrong side.

Silk ends give a book a rich finish, but seldom look altogether satisfactory. If the silk is merely stuck on to the first end paper, the edges will generally fray out if the book is much used. If the edges are turned in, an unpleasantly thick end is made.

Leather Joints

Leather joints are pieces of thin leather that are used to cover the joints on the inside (for paring, see page 154). They add very little strength to the book, but give a pleasant finish to the inside of the board.

If there are to be leather joints, the end papers are made up without A1, and the edge of the leather pasted and inserted at D, with a piece of common paper as a protection (see fig. 19, IV). When the paste is dry, the leather is folded over at E.

A piece of blotting-paper may be pasted on to the inside of the waste leaf, leaving enough of it loose to go between the leather joint and the first sheet of the end paper. This will avoid any chance of the leather joint staining or marking the ends while the book is being bound. The blotting-paper, of course, is taken out with the waste sheet before the joint is pasted down.

Joints may also be made of linen or cloth inserted in the same way. A cloth joint has greater strength than a leather one, as the latter has to be very thin in order that the board may shut properly.

Leather Joints

With leather or cloth joints, the sewing should go through both E and F.

PRESSING

Pressing

While the end papers are being made, the sections of the book should be pressed. To do this a pressing-board is taken

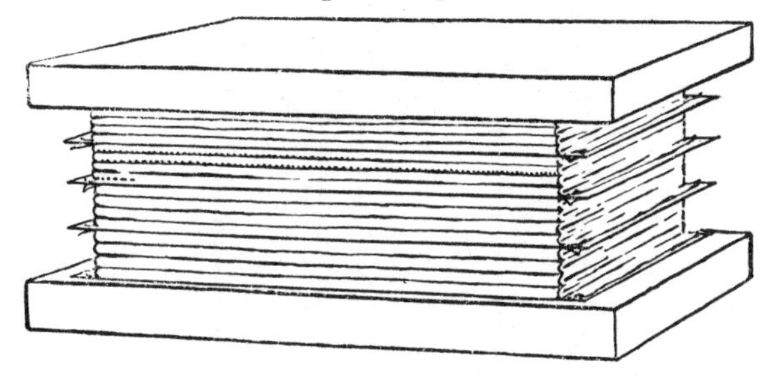

FIG. 20

which is a little larger than the book, and a tin, covered with common paper, placed on that, then a few sections of the book, then another tin covered with paper, and then more sections, and so on, taking care that the sections are exactly over one another (see fig. 20). A second pressing-board having been placed on the last tin

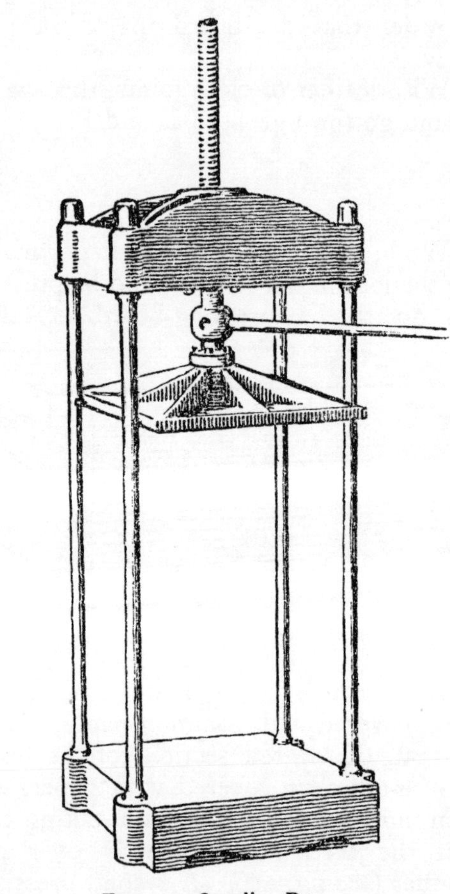

FIG. 21.—Standing Press

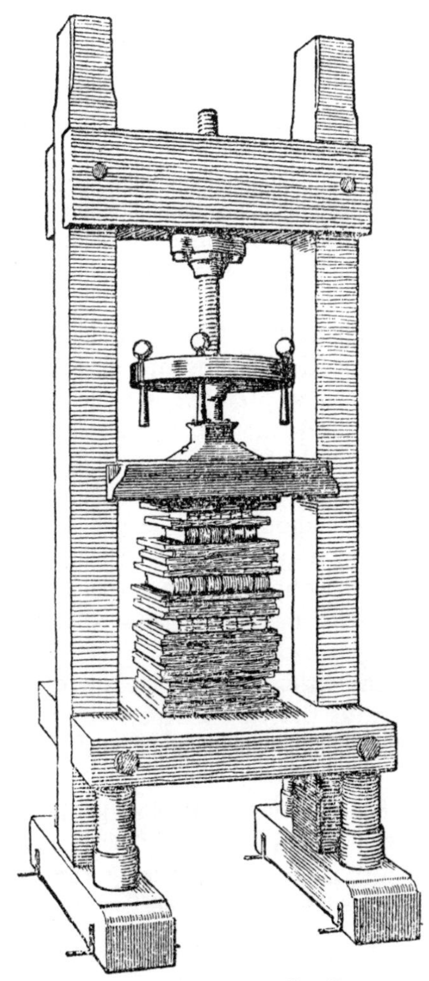

FIG. 22.—French Standing Press

Pressing

the pile of sections, tins, and pressing-boards can be put into the standing press and left under pressure till next day. Newly printed plates should be protected by thin tissue paper while being pressed. Any folded plates or maps, &c., or inserted letters, must either not be pressed, or have tins placed on each side of them to prevent them from indenting the adjoining leaves.

Hand-printed books, such as the publications of the Kelmscott Press, should have very little pressure, or the "impression" of the print and the surface of the paper may be injured. Books newly printed on vellum or heavily coloured illustrations should not be pressed at all, or the print may "set off."

The protecting tissues on the plates of a book that has been printed for more than a year can generally be left out, unless the titles of the plates are printed on them, as they are a nuisance to readers and often get crumpled up and mark the book.

In order to make books solid, that is, to make the leaves lie evenly and closely to one another, it was formerly the custom to beat books on a "stone" with a heavy hammer. This process has been superseded by the rolling-press; but with the admirable presses that are now to be had, simple pressing will be found to be sufficient for the "extra" binder.

Pressing

At fig. 21 is shown an iron standing press. This is screwed down first with a short bar, and finally with a long bar. This form of press is effective and simple, but needs a good deal of room for the long bar, and must have very firm supports or it may be pulled over.

At fig. 22 is shown a French standing press, in which the pressure is applied by a weighted wheel, which will, in the first place, by being spun round, turn the screw until it is tight, and give additional pressure by a hammering action. This press I have found to answer for all ordinary purposes, and to give as great pressure as can be got by the iron standing press, without any undue strain on supports or workmen.

There are many other forms of press by which great pressure can be applied, some working by various arrangements of cog-wheels, screws, and levers, others by hydraulic pressure.

CHAPTER VI

Trimming Edges before Sewing—Edge Gilding

TRIMMING BEFORE SEWING

Trimming before Sewing

WHEN the sheets come from the press the treatment of the edges must be decided upon, that is, whether they are to be entirely uncut, trimmed before sewing, or cut in boards.

Early printed books and manuscripts should on no account have their edges cut at all, and any modern books of value are better only slightly trimmed and gilt before sewing. But for books of reference that need good bindings, on account of the wear they have to withstand, cutting in boards is best, as the smooth edge so obtained makes the leaves easier to turn over. Gilt tops and rough edges give a book a look of unequal finish.

If the edges are to remain uncut, or be cut "in boards" with the plough, the book will be ready for "marking up" as soon as it comes from the press; but if it is to be gilt before sewing, it must first be trimmed.

The sheets for trimming with end papers and all plates inserted must first be cut square at the head against a carpenter's square (see fig. 7). Then a piece of mill-board may be cut to the size it is desired to leave the leaves, and the sections trimmed to it. To do this three nails should be put into the covering board through a piece of straw-board, and the back of the section slid along nails 1 and 2 until it touches No. 3 (see fig. 23). The board is slid in the same way, and anything projecting beyond it cut off. When the under straw-board has become inconveniently scored in the first position, by shifting the lower nail (1) a fresh surface will receive the cuts. Fig. 24 is a representation of a simple machine that I use in my workshop for trimming. The slides A A are adjustable to any width required, and are fixed by the screws B B.

Trimming before Sewing

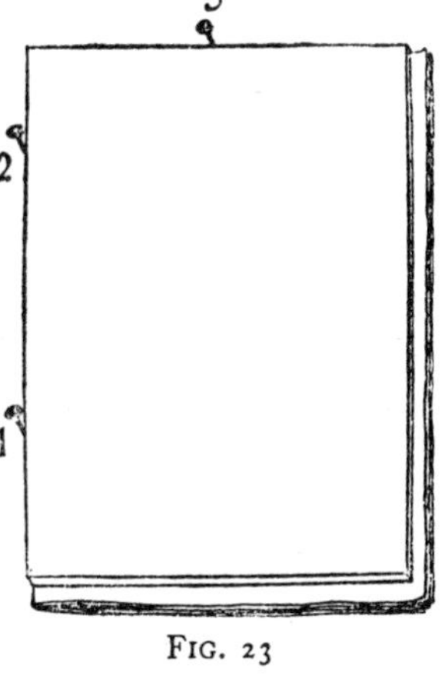

FIG. 23

Trimming before Sewing

The brass-bound straight edge C fits on to slots in A A, and as this, by the adjustment of the slides, can be fixed at any distance from B B, all sizes of books can be trimmed. As by this machine several sections can be cut at once, the time taken

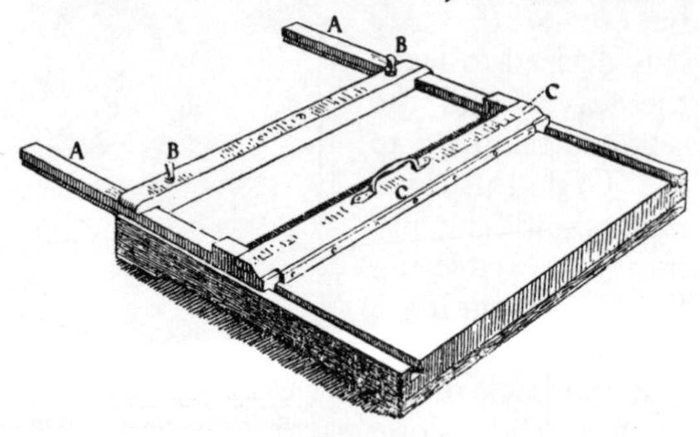

FIG. 24

is not very much greater than if the book were cut in the plough.

Considerable judgment is required in trimming. The edges of the larger pages only, on a previously uncut book, should be cut, leaving the smaller pages untouched. Such uncut pages are called "proof," and the existence of proof in a bound book is evidence that it has not been unduly cut.

Before gilding the edges of the trimmed

sections, any uncut folds that may remain should be opened with a folder, as if opened after gilding they will show a ragged white edge.

Trimming before Sewing

EDGE GILDING

Edge Gilding

To gild the edges of trimmed sections, the book must be "knocked up" to the fore-edge, getting as many of the short leaves as possible to the front. It is then put into the "lying press," with gilding boards on each side (see fig. 25), and screwed up tightly. Very little scraping will be necessary, and usually if well rubbed with fine sand-paper, to remove any chance finger-marks or loose fragments of paper, the edge will be smooth enough to gild. If the paper is very absorbent, the edges must be washed over with vellum size and left to dry.

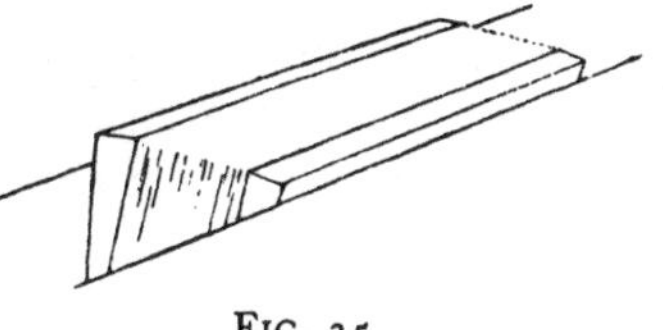

FIG. 25

The next process is an application of red chalk. For this a piece of gilder's red chalk is rubbed down on a stone with water, making a thickish paste, and the edges are well brushed with a hard brush dipped in this mixture, care being taken not to have it wet enough to run between the leaves. Some gilders prefer to use blacklead or a mixture of chalk and black-lead. A further brushing with a dry brush will to some extent polish the leaves. It will then be ready for an application of glaire. Before glairing, the gold must be cut on the cushion to the width required (see p. 200), and may be taken up either on very slightly greased paper, a gilder's tip, or with a piece of net stretched on a little frame (see fig. 26). The gold leaf will adhere sufficiently to the net, and can be readily released by a light breath when it is exactly over the proper place on the edge.

When the gold is ready, the glaire should be floated on to the edge with a soft brush, and the gold laid evenly over it and left until dry; that is, in a workshop of ordinary temperature, for about an hour. The edge is then lightly rubbed with a piece of leather that has been previously rubbed on beeswax, and is ready for burnishing. It is best to commence burnishing through a piece of thin slightly waxed paper to set the gold, and afterwards the burnisher can be used

Edge Gilding

FIG. 26

directly on the edge. A piece of bloodstone ground so as to have no sharp edges (see fig. 27) makes a good burnisher.

There are several different preparations used for gilding edges. One part of

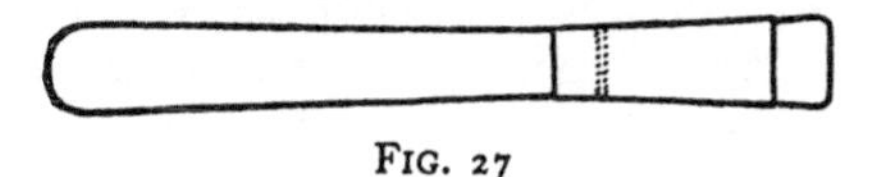

FIG. 27

beaten up white of egg with four parts of water left to stand for a day and strained will be found to answer well.

Edge Gilding

After the fore-edge is gilt the same operation is repeated at the head and tail. As it is desirable to have the gilding at the head as solid as possible, rather more scraping is advisable here, or the head may be left to be cut with a plough and gilt in boards.

CHAPTER VII

Marking Up—Sewing—Materials for Sewing

MARKING UP

Marking Up

THIS is drawing lines across the back of the sections to show the sewer the position of the sewing cords.

Marking up for flexible sewing needs care and judgment, as on it depends the position of the bands on the back of the bound book. Nearly all books look best with five bands, but very large, thinnish folios may have six, and a very small, thick book may look better with four. Generally speaking, five is the best number. In marking up trimmed sheets for flexible sewing, the length of the back should be divided from the head into six portions, five equal, and one at the tail slightly longer. From the points so arrived at, strong pencil lines should be made across the back with a carpenter's square as guide, the book having been previously knocked up between pressing-boards, and placed in the lying press. It is important that the head should be knocked up exactly square, as otherwise the bands will be found to slope when the book is bound. In the case of a book which is to be cut and gilt in boards, before marking up it will be necessary to decide how much is to be cut off, and allowance made, or the head and tail division of the back will, when cut, be too small. It must also be remembered that to the height of the pages the amount of the "squares" will be added.

Marking Up

About a quarter of an inch from either end of the back of a trimmed book, and a little more in the case of one that is to be cut in boards, a mark should be made for the "kettle" or "catch" stitch. This may be slightly sawn in, but before using the saw, the end papers are removed. If these were sawn, the holes would show in the joint when the ends are pasted down.

If the book is to be sewn on double

Marking Up

cords, or on slips of vellum or tape, two lines will be necessary for each band.

It has become the custom to saw in the backs of books, and to sink the bands into the saw cuts, using "hollow backs," and putting false bands to appear when bound. This is a degenerate form, to which is due much of the want of durability of modern bindings. If the bands are not to show on the back, it is better to sew on tapes or strips of vellum than to use sawn-in string bands.

SEWING

Sewing

The sewing-frame used by bookbinders is practically the same now as is shown in prints of the early sixteenth century, and probably dates from still earlier times. It consists of a bed with two uprights and a crossbar, which can be heightened or lowered by the turning of wooden nuts working on a screw thread cut in the uprights (see fig. 29).

To set up for sewing, as many loops of cord, called "lay cords," as there are to be bands, are threaded on to the cross piece, and to these, by a simple knot, shown at fig. 28, cords are fastened to form the bands. The "lay cords"

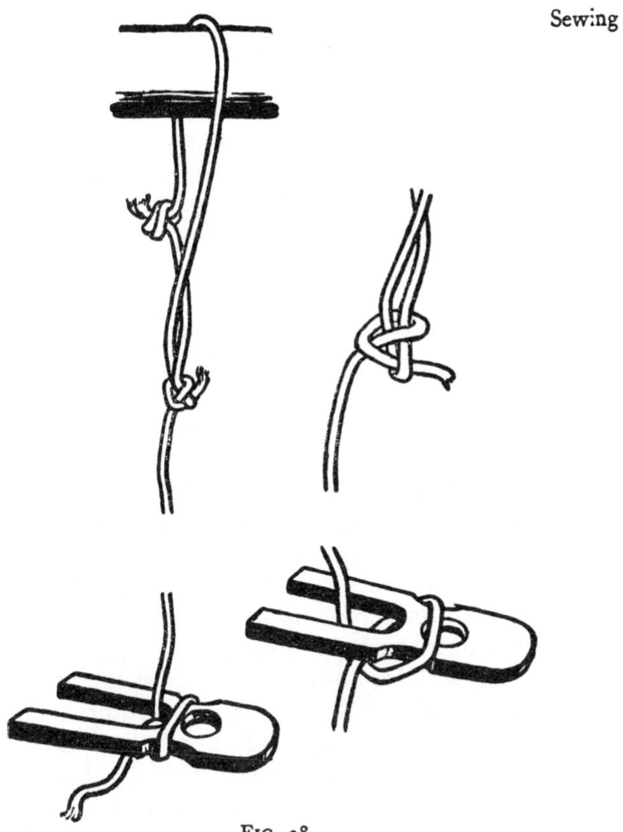

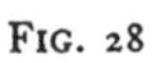

FIG. 28

can be used again and again until worn out.

To fasten the cord below, a key is taken (see fig. 28) and held below the press by the right hand; the cord is then pulled up round it by the left, and held in position on the key by the first finger of the right hand. The key is then turned over, winding up a little of the string, and the prongs slipped over the main cord. It is then put through the slit in the bed of the sewing-press, with the prongs away from the front. The cord is then cut off, and the same operation repeated for each band. When all the bands have been set up, the book is laid against them, and they are moved to correspond with the marks previously made on the back of the book, care being taken that they are quite perpendicular. If they are of the same length and evenly set up, on screwing up the crossbar they should all tighten equally.

It will be found to be convenient to set up the cords as far to the right hand of the press as possible, as then there will be room for the sewer's left arm on the inner side of the left hand upright.

A roll of paper that will exactly fill the slot in the sewing-frame is pushed in in front of the upright cords to steady them and ensure that they are all in the same plane.

When the sewing-frame is ready, with the cords set up and adjusted, the book must be collated to make sure that neither sheets nor plates have been lost or misplaced during the previous operations. Plates need special care to see that the guards go properly round the sheets next them.

The top back corner, on front and back waste end paper, should be marked. When this has been done, and all is found to be in order, the book is laid on a pressing-board behind the sewing-frame, the fore-edge towards the sewer, and the front end paper uppermost. As it is difficult to insert the needle into a section placed on the bed of the sewing-frame, it will be found convenient to sew upon a largish pressing-board, which will lie on the bed of the frame, and may have small catches to prevent it from shifting. When the board is in place, the first section (end paper) is taken in the left hand and turned over, so that the marks on the back come in the proper places against the strings. The left hand is inserted into the place where the sewing is to be, and with the right hand a needle and thread are passed through the kettle stitch

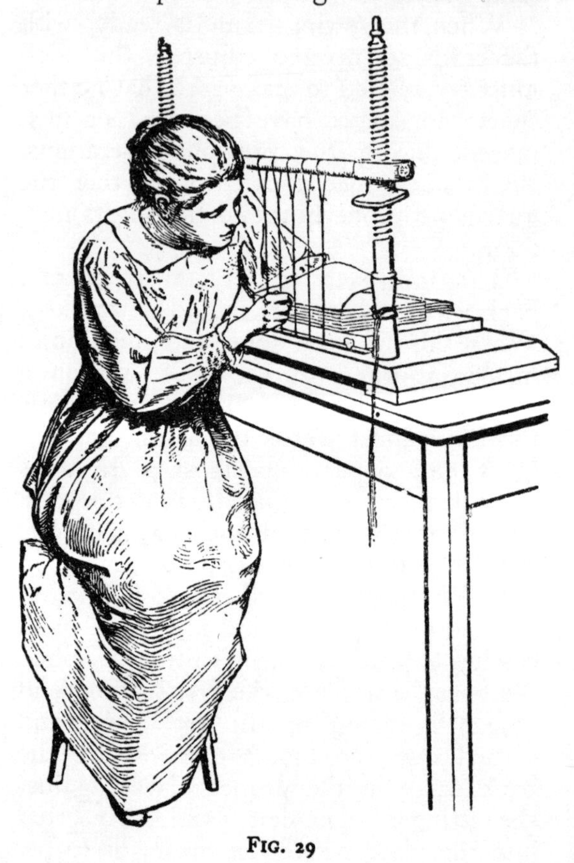

FIG. 29

mark (see fig. 29). The needle is grasped by the fingers of the left hand, is passed out through the back at the first mark on the left-hand side of the first upright cord, and pulled tight, leaving a loose end of thread at the kettle stitch. Then with

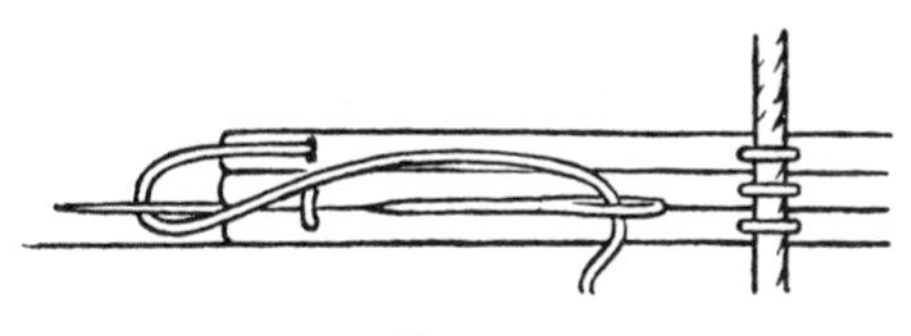

FIG. 30

the right hand it is inserted again in the same place, but from the other side of the cord, and so on round all five bands, and out again at the kettle stitch mark at the tail, using right and left hands alternately. The centre of the next section is then found, and it is sewn in the same way from tail to head, the thread being tied to the loose end hanging from the first kettle stitch. Another section is laid on and sewn, but when the kettle stitch is reached, the under thread is caught up in the way shown in fig. 30. These operations are repeated throughout the whole book. If the back seems likely to swell too much, the sections can

Sewing

be lightly tapped down with a loaded stick made for the purpose, care being taken not to drive the sections inwards as it is difficult to get such sections out again. When all the sheets and the last end paper have been sewn on, a double catch stitch is made, and the end cut off. This method is known as flexible sewing "all along."

When one needle full of thread is exhausted, another is tied on, making practically a continuous length of thread going all along each section and round every band. The weaver's knot is the best for joining the lengths of thread. A simple way of tying it is shown at fig. 31. A simple slip knot is made in the end of the new thread and put over the end of the old, and, on being pulled tight, the old thread should slip through, as shewn at B. The convenience of this knot is that by its use a firm attachment can be made quite close up to the back of the

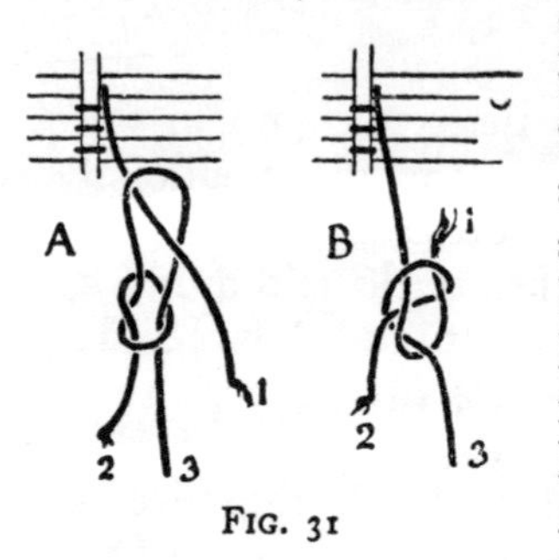

FIG. 31

book. This is a great advantage, as if the knot is made at some distance from the back, it will have to be dragged through the section two or three times, instead of only once. The knot, after having been made, must be pulled inside the section, and remain there. Considerable judgment is required in sewing. If a book is sewn too loosely, it is almost impossible to bind it firmly; and if too tightly, especially if the kettle stitches have been drawn too tight, the thread may break in "backing," and the book have to be resewn.

One way to avoid having too much swelling in the back of a book consisting of a great many very thin sections is to sew "two sheets on." In this form of sewing two sections at a time are laid on the sewing-frame. The thread is inserted at the "kettle stitch" of the lower section, and brought out as usual at the first cord, but instead of being reinserted into the lower section, it is passed into the upper one, and so on, alternately passing into the upper and lower sections. This will give, if there are five bands, three stitches in each section instead of six, as there would be if the sewing were "all along," lessening the thread, consequently the swelling, by half. It is usual to sew the first and last few sections "all along."

The common method of sewing is to make saw cuts in the back, in which thin cords can be sunk, and the thread merely passes behind them and not around them, as in flexible sewing. This method, although very quick and cheap, is not to be recommended, on account of the injury done to the backs of the sections by the saw, and because the glue running into the saw cuts is apt to make the back stiff, and to prevent the book from opening right to the back. Indeed, were a sawn-in book to open right to the back, as it is expected a flexibly-sewn book will do, showing the sewing along the centre of each section, the saw marks with the band inserted would show, and be a serious disfigurement.

Mediæval books were usually sewn on double cords or strips of leather, and the headband was often sewn at the same time, as shown at fig. 32, A. This is an excellent method for very large books with heavy sections, and is specially suitable for large vellum manuscripts, in many of which the sections are very thick. An advantage of this method is that the twist round the double cord virtually makes a knot at every band, and should a thread at any place break, there is no danger of the rest of the thread coming loose. This is the only mode of sewing by which a thread runs absolutely from end to end of the sections. The headband sewn at the same time, and so tied down in every section, is firmer and stronger than if worked on in the way now usual. In the fifteenth century it was the custom to lace the ends of the headbands into the boards in the same way as the other bands. This method, while giving additional strength at the head and tail, and avoiding the somewhat unfinished look of the cut-off ends of the modern headband, is, on the whole, of doubtful advantage, as it is necessary to cut the "turn in" at the point where strength in the leather is much wanted.

At fig. 32 is shown in section the three methods of sewing mentioned. A is the old sewing round double bands; with the headbands worked at the same time with the same thread; B is the modern flexible sewing, and C the common sawn-in method.

Books that are very thin or are to be

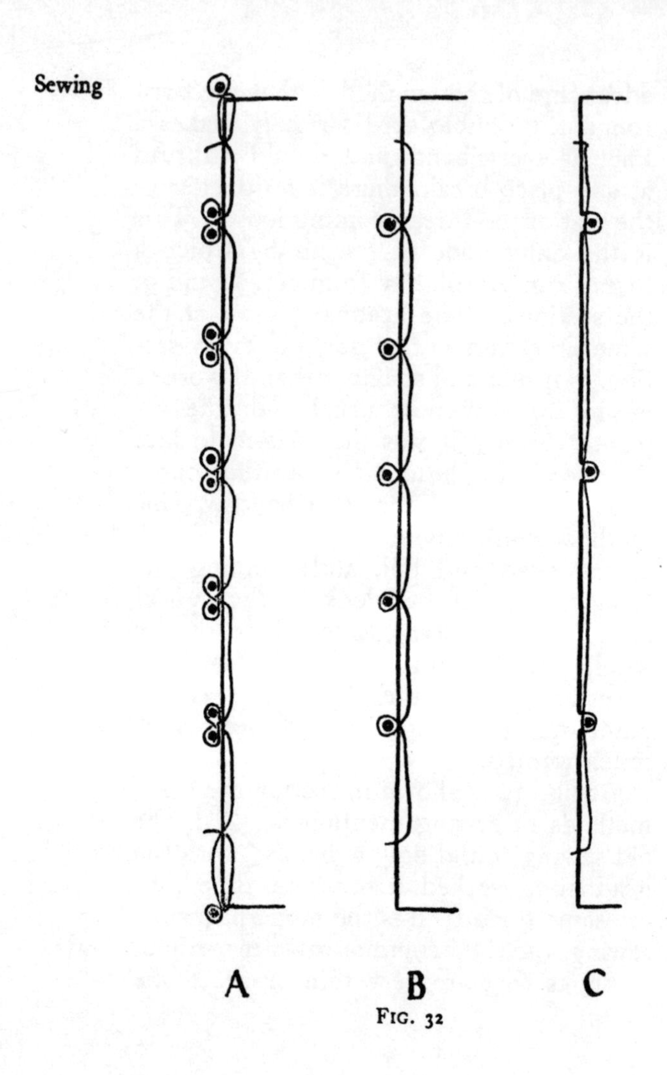

FIG. 32

Sewing

bound in vellum, are best sewn on tapes or vellum slips. The easiest way to set up the sewing-frame for such sewing is to sling a piece of wood through two of the lay cords, and to pin one end of the vellum or tape band round this, pull the other end tight, and secure it with a drawing-pin underneath the frame. The sewing, in the case of such flat bands, would not go round, but only across them. To avoid undue looseness, every three or four threads may be caught up at the back of the band, as shown in fig. 33.

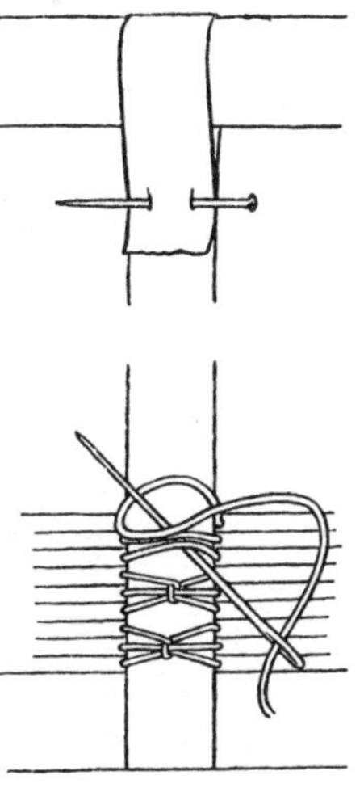

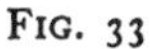

Fig. 33

MATERIALS FOR SEWING

Materials for Sewing

The cord used should be of the best hemp, specially made with only two strands of very long fibres to facilitate fraying out. For very large books where a double cord is to be used, the best water line will be found to answer, care being taken to select that which can be frayed out. If tape is used it should be unbleached, such as the sailmakers use. Thread should also be unbleached, as the unnecessary bleaching of most bookbinder's sewing-thread seems to cause it to rot in a comparatively short time. Silk of the best quality is better than any thread. The ligature silk, undyed, as used by surgeons, is perhaps the strongest material, and can be had in various thicknesses. It is impossible to pay too great attention to the selection of sewing materials, as the permanency of the binding depends on their durability. The rebinding of valuable books is at best a necessary evil, and anything that makes frequent rebinding necessary is not only objectionable on account of the cost involved, but because it seriously shortens the life of the book.

Experience is required to judge what thickness of thread to use for any given book. If the sections are very thin, a thin thread must be used, or the "swelling" of the back caused by the additional thickness of the thread in that part will be excessive, and make the book unmanageable in "backing." On the other hand, if the sections are large, and a too thin thread is used, there will not be enough swelling to make a firm "joint." Broadly speaking, when there are a great many very thin sections, the thinnest thread may be used; and coarser thread may be used when the sections are thicker, or fewer in number. In the case of large manuscripts on vellum it is best to use very thick silk, or even catgut. Vellum is so tough and durable, that any binding of a vellum book should be made as if it were expected to last for hundreds of years.

In selecting the thickness of cord for a book, some judgment is required. On an old book the bands are best made rather prominent by the use of thick cord, but the exact thickness to be used is a matter for taste and experience to decide.

A very thick band on a small book is clumsy, while a very thin band on the back of a heavy book suggests weakness, and is therefore unsightly.

In bindings of early printed books and manuscripts an appearance of great strength is better than extreme neatness.

When the sewing is completed, the cords are cut off close to the lay cords, and then

Materials for Sewing

the keys will be loose enough to be easily removed. The knots remaining on the lay bands are removed, and the keys slung through one of them.

CHAPTER VIII

Fraying Out Slips—Gluing Up—Rounding and Backing

FRAYING OUT SLIPS AND GLUING UP

Fraying Out Slips and Gluing Up

AFTER sewing, the book should be looked through to see that all sheets and plates have been caught by the thread, and special attention should be given to end papers to see that the sewing lies evenly.

The ends of the cords should next be cut off to within about two inches of the book on each side, and the free portions frayed out. If proper sewing cord is used, this will be found to be very easily done, if a binder's bodkin is first inserted between the two strands, separating them, and then again in the centre of each separated strand to straighten the fibres still further (see fig. 34).

The fraying out of the thick cord

Fraying Out Slips and Gluing Up

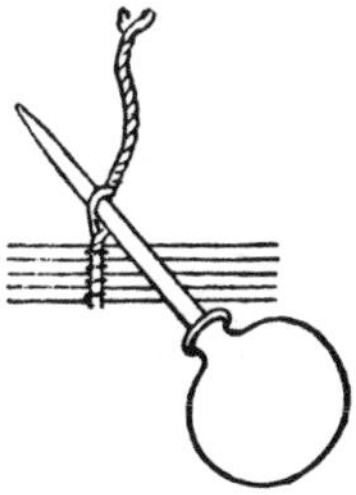

recommended for heavy books is a more difficult operation, but with a little trouble the fibres of any good cord can be frayed out. Vellum or tape bands will only require cutting off, leaving about two inches free on each side. The free parts of the bands are called slips.

FIG. 34

The book is now ready for gluing up. A piece of waste mill-board or an old cloth cover is put on each side over the slips, and the book knocked up squarely at the back and head. Then it is lowered into the lying press and screwed up, leaving the back with the protecting boards projecting about three-quarters of an inch. If the back has too much swelling in it or is spongy, it is better to leave the slips on one side free and to pull them as tight as possible while the book is held in the press, or a knocking-down iron may be placed on one side of the projecting back and the other side tapped with the backing hammer to make the sections lie close to one another, and then the slips pulled straight (fig. 35). The back must

Fraying Out Slips and Gluing Up

now be glued. The glue for this operation must be hot, and not too thick. It is very important that it should be worked well between the sections with the brush, and it is well after it has been applied to rub the back with a finger or folder to

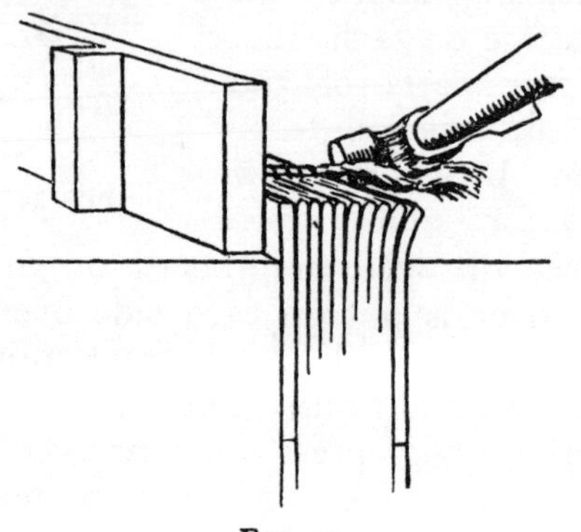

FIG. 35

make quite sure that the glue goes between every section for its entire length. If the book is too tightly screwed up in the press, the glue is apt to remain too much on the surface; and if not tightly enough, it may penetrate too deeply between the sections. If the glue is thick, or stringy, it may be diluted with hot water and the glue-brush rapidly spun round in the glue-pot to break it up and to make it work freely.

Fraying Out Slips and Gluing Up

Very great care is needed to see that the head of a previously trimmed book is knocked up exactly square before the back is glued, for if it is not, it will be very difficult to get it even afterwards.

ROUNDING AND BACKING

Rounding and Backing

The amount of rounding on the back of a book should be determined by the necessities of the case; that is to say, a back that has through guarding, or excess of sewing, a tendency to be round, is best not forced to be flat, and a back that would naturally be flat, is best not forced to be unduly round. A very round back is objectionable where it can be avoided, because it takes up so much of the back margins of the sheets, and is apt to make the book stiff in opening. On the other hand, a back that is quite flat has to be lined up stiffly, or it may become concave with use.

The method of rounding is to place the book with the back projecting a little over the edge of the press or table, then to draw the back over towards the workman, and, while in this position, to tap it carefully with a hammer (see fig. 36). This is repeated on the other side of the book, and, if properly done, will give

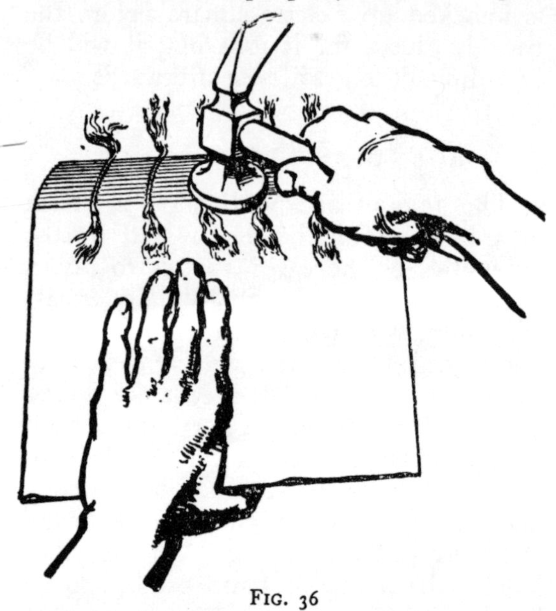

FIG. 36

the back an even, convex form that should be, in section, a portion of a circle. Rounding and backing are best done after the glue has ceased to be tacky, but before it has set hard.

Rounding and Backing

Backing is perhaps the most difficult and important operation in forwarding. The sewing threads in the back cause that part to be thicker than the rest of the book. Thus in a book with twenty sections there will be in the back, in addition to

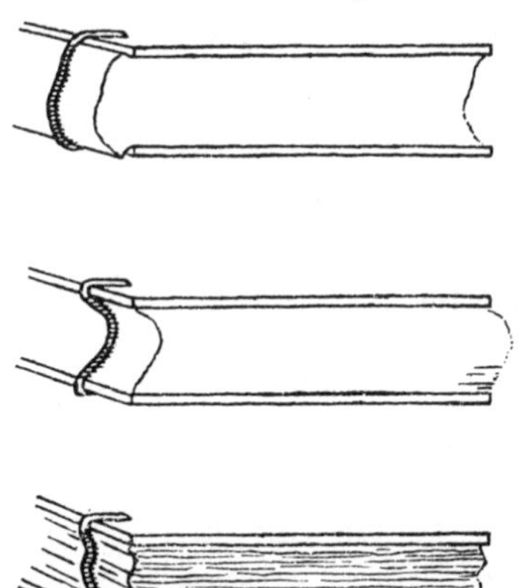

FIG. 37

the thickness of the paper, twenty thicknesses of thread.

If the boards were laced on to the book without rounding or backing, and the book were pressed, the additional thickness of the back, having to go somewhere, would cause it to go either convex or concave, or else perhaps to crease up

Rounding and Backing

(see fig. 37). The object of rounding is to control the distribution of this swelling, and to make the back take an even and permanently convex form.

If the boards were merely laced on after rounding, there would be a gap between the square ends of the board and the edge of the back (see fig. 38), though the convexity and even curve of the back would be to some extent assured. What is done in backing is to make a groove, into which the edges of the board will fit neatly, and to hammer the backs of the sections over one another from the centre outwards on both sides to form the "groove," to ensure that the back shall return to the same form after the book has been opened.

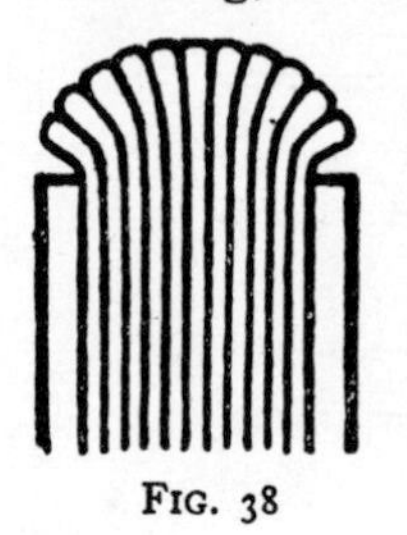

Fig. 38

To back the book, backing boards are placed on each side (leaving the slips outside) a short distance below the edge to the back (fig. 39). The amount to leave here must be decided by the thickness of the boards to be used. When the backing

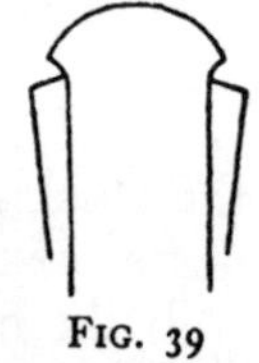

Fig. 39

Rounding and Backing

boards are in position, the book and boards must be carefully lowered into the lying press and screwed up very tightly, great care being taken to see that the boards do not slip, and that the book is put in evenly. Even the most experienced forwarder will sometimes have to take a book out of the press two or three times

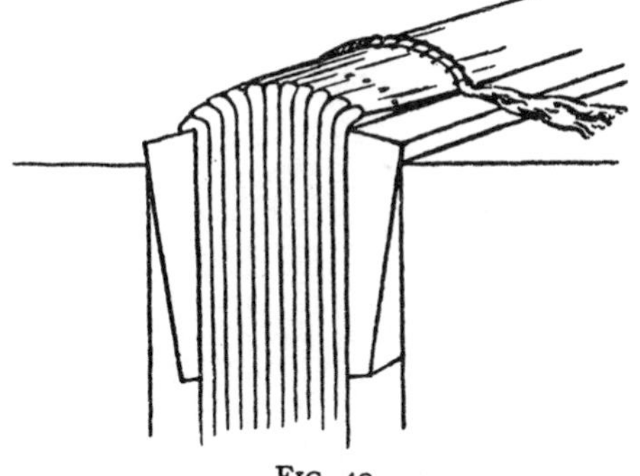

FIG. 40

before he gets it in quite evenly and without allowing the boards to slip. Unless the back has a perfectly even curve when put in the press for backing, no amount of subsequent hammering will put it permanently right.

The backs of the sections should be evenly fanned out one over the other from the centre outwards on both sides.

Rounding and Backing

This is done by side strokes of the hammer, in fact by a sort of "riveting" blow, and not by a directly crushing blow (see fig. 41, in which the arrows show the direction of the hammer strokes). If the sections are not evenly fanned out from

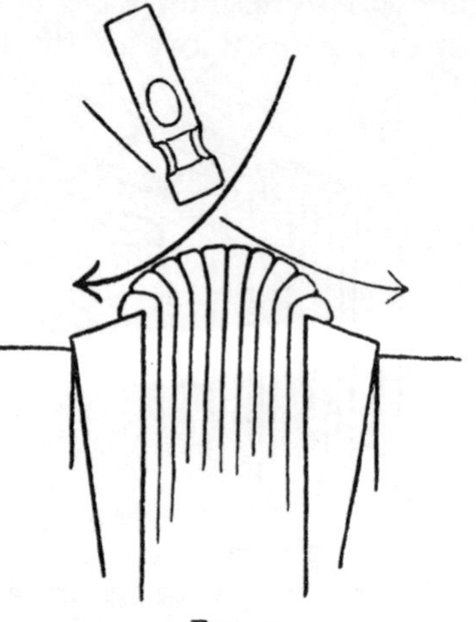

FIG. 41

the centre, but are either zigzagged by being crushed by direct blows of the hammer, as shown in fig. 42, A, or are unevenly fanned over more to one side than the other, as shown in fig. 42, B, the back, although it may be even enough when first done, will probably become uneven with use. A book in which the sections have been crushed down, as at fig. 42, A, will be disfigured inside by creases in the paper.

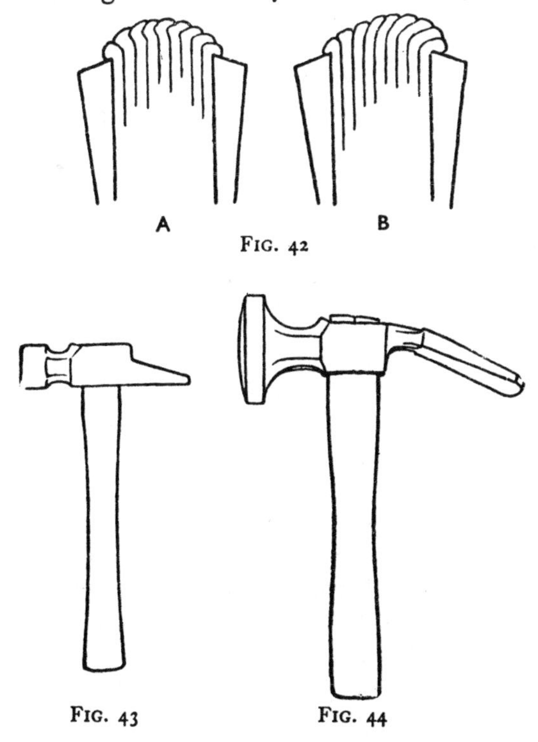

FIG. 42

FIG. 43

FIG. 44

It is a mistake to suppose that a very heavy hammer is necessary for backing

Rounding and Backing

any but the largest books. For flexible books a hammer with a comparatively small face should be used, as by its use the book can be backed without flattening the bands. It is well to have a hammer head of the shape shown in fig. 43. By using the thin end, the force of a comparatively light blow, because concentrated on a small surface, is effective.

At fig. 44 is shown an ordinary backing hammer.

CHAPTER IX

Cutting and Attaching Boards—Cleaning off Back—Pressing

CUTTING AND ATTACHING BOARDS

Cutting and Attaching Boards

THE first quality of the best black board made from old rope is the best to use for "extra" binding. It will be found to be very hard, and not easily broken or bent at the corners. In selecting the thickness suitable for any given book, the size and thickness of the volume should be taken into account. The tendency of most modern binders is to use a rather over thick board, perhaps with a view to bulk out the volume. For manuscripts, or other books on vellum, it is best to use wooden boards, which should be clasped. From their stability they form a kind of permanent press, in which the vellum leaves are kept flat. In a damp climate like that of England, vellum, absorbing moisture from the atmosphere, soon cockles up unless it is held tightly in some way; and when it is once cockled, the book cannot be made to shut properly, except with very special treatment. Then also dust and damp have ready access to the interstices of the crinkled pages, resulting in the disfigurement so well known and so deplored by all lovers of fine books.

For large books a "made" board, that is, two boards pasted together, is better than a single board of the same thickness. In making boards a thin and a thick board should be pasted together, the thin board to go nearer the book. It will not be necessary to put a double lining on the inside of such boards, as a thin board will always draw a thick one.

If mill-boards are used they are first cut roughly to size with the mill-board

Cutting and Attaching Boards

shears, screwed up in the "lying" press. The straight arm of the shears is the one to fix in the press, for if the bent arm be undermost, the knuckles are apt to be

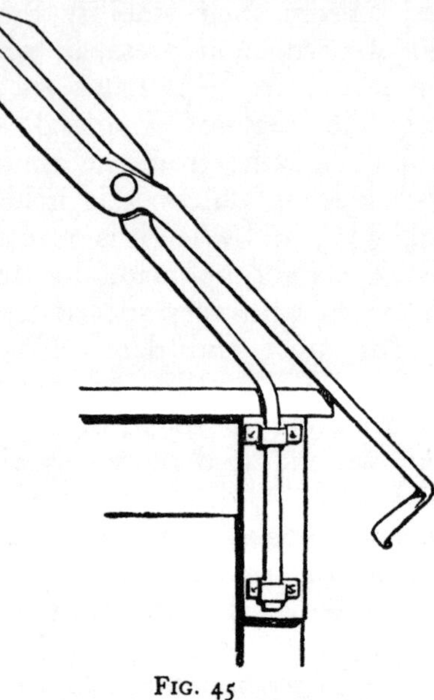

FIG. 45

severely bruised against the end. A better way of fixing the shears is shown at fig. 45. Any blacksmith will bend the arm of the shears and make the necessary clips. This method saves trouble and considerable wear and tear to the "lying" press. Where a great many boards are needed, they may be quickly cut in a board machine, but for "extra" work they should be further trimmed in the plough, in the same way as those cut by the shears. After the boards have been roughly cut to size, they should have one edge cut straight with the plough. To do this one or two pairs of boards are knocked up to the back and inserted in the cutting side of the press, with those edges projecting which are to be cut off, and behind them, as a "cut against," a board protected by a waste piece of mill-board.

The plough, held by the screw and handle, and guided by the runners on the press, is moved backwards and forwards. A slight turn of the screw at each movement brings the knife forward. In cutting mill-boards which are very hard, the screw should be turned very little each time. If press and plough are in proper order, that part of the board which projects above the cheek of the press should be cut off, leaving the edges perfectly square and straight. If the edge of the press has been damaged, or is out of "truth," a cutting board may be used between the cheek of the press and the board to be

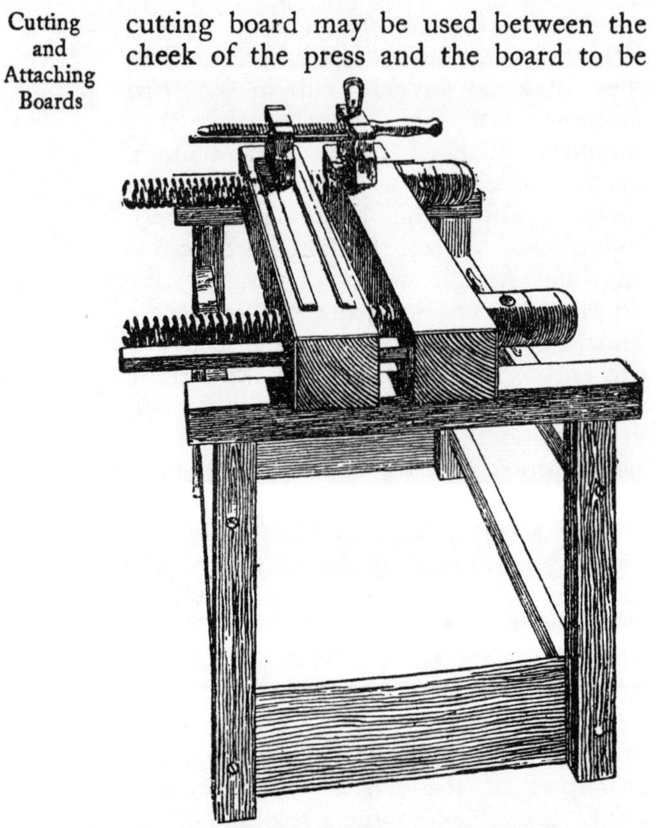

FIG. 46.—Lying or Cutting Press

cut, making a true edge for the knife to run on.

The position of the plough on the press is shown at fig. 46. The side of the press with runners should be reserved for cutting, the other side used for all other work.

Cutting and Attaching Boards

The plough knife for mill-boards should not be ground at too acute an angle, or the edge will most likely break away at the first cut. The shape shown at fig. 47 is suitable. The knife should be very frequently ground, as it soon gets blunt, which adds greatly to the labour of cutting.

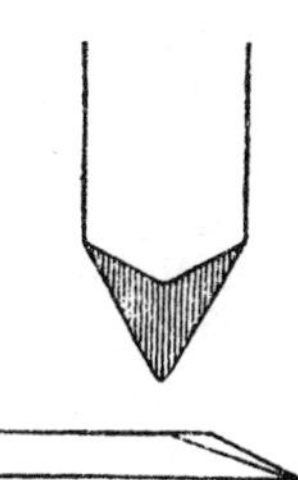

FIG. 47

After an edge has been cut, each side should be well rubbed with a folder to smooth down any burr left by the plough knife. Then a piece of common paper with one edge cut straight is pasted on to one side of the board, with the straight edge exactly up to the cut edge of the board. Then a piece of paper large enough to cover both sides of the board is pasted round it, and well rubbed down at the cut edge. After having been lined, the boards are nipped in the press to ensure that the lining paper shall stick.

They are stood up to dry, with the doubly lined side outwards. The double paper is intended to warp the board slightly to that side, to compensate for the pull of the leather when the book is covered. If the board is a double one, a single lining paper will be sufficient, the thinner board helping to draw the thicker. The paste for lining boards must be fairly thin, and very well beaten up so as to be free from lumps. It is of the utmost importance that the lining papers should stick properly, for unless they stick, no subsequent covering of leather or paper can be made to lie flat.

When the lined boards are quite dry, they should be paired with the doubly lined sides together, and the top back corner marked to correspond with the marks on the top back corners of the book. Then near the top edge, with the aid of a carpenter's square, two points are marked in a line at right angles to the cut edge. The pair of boards is then knocked up to the back and lowered into the press as before, so that the plough knife will exactly cut through the points. The same operation is repeated on the two remaining uncut edges. In marking out those for the fore-edge, the measurement is taken with a pair of compasses (fig. 48) from the joint of the book to the fore-edge of the first section. If the book has been trimmed, or is to remain uncut, a little more must be allowed for the "squares," and if it is to be cut in the plough, it must now be decided how much is to be cut off, remembering that it is much better to have the boards a little too large, and so have to reduce them after the book is cut, than to have them too small, and either be obliged to get out a new pair of boards, or unduly cut down the book.

FIG. 48

The height of the boards for a book that has been trimmed, or is to remain uncut, will be the height of the page with a small allowance at each end for the squares. When a pair of boards has been cut all round, it can be tested for squareness by reversing one board, when any inequality that there may be will appear doubled. If the boards are out of truth they should generally be put on one side, to be used for a smaller book, and new boards got out. To correct a badly cut pair of boards, it is necessary to reduce them in size, and the book consequently suffers in proportion. If the boards have been found to be truly cut, they are laid on the book, and the position of the slips marked on them by lines at right angles to the back. A line is then made parallel to the back, about half an inch in (see fig. 49). At the points where the lines cross, a series of holes is punched from the front with a binder's bodkin on a lead plate, then the board is turned over, and a second series is punched from the back about half an inch from the first. If the groove of the back is shallower than the thickness of the board, the top back edge of the board should be bevelled off with a file. This will not be necessary if the groove is the exact depth. When the holes have been punched, it is well to cut a series of V-shaped depressions from the first series of holes to the back to receive

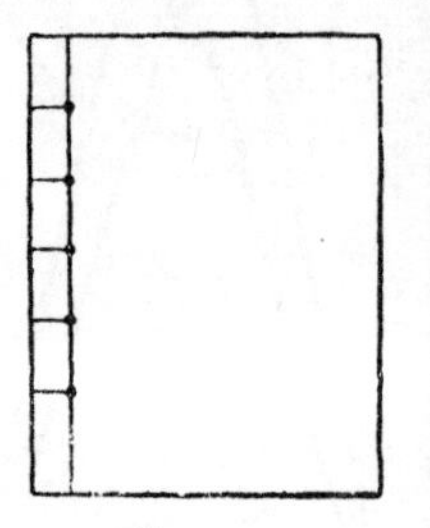

FIG. 49

the slips, or they may be too prominent when the book is bound. It will now be necessary considerably to reduce the slips that were frayed out after sewing, and to remove all glue or any other matter attached to them. The extent to which they may be reduced is a matter of nice judgment. In the desire to ensure absolute neatness in the covering, modern binders often reduce the slips to almost nothing. On the other hand, some go to the other extreme, and leave the cord entire, making great ridges on the sides of the book where it is laced in. It should be possible with the aid of the depressions, cut as described, to use slips with sufficient margin of strength, and yet to have no undue projection on the cover. A slight projection is not unsightly, as it gives an assurance of sound construction and strength, and, moreover, makes an excellent starting-point for any pattern that may be used. When the slips have been scraped and reduced, the portion left should consist of long straight silky fibres. These must be well pasted, and the ends very slightly twisted. The pointed ends are then threaded through the first series of holes in the front of the board, and

Cutting and Attaching Boards

back again through the second (fig. 50). In lacing in the slips must not be pulled so tight as to prevent the board from shutting freely, nor left so loose as to make a perceptible interval in the joint of

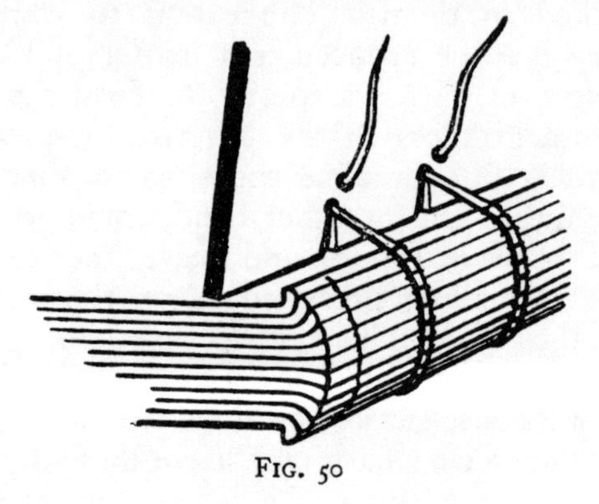

FIG. 50

the book. The pasted slips having been laced in, their ends are cut off with a sharp knife, flush with the surface of the board. The laced-in slips are then well hammered on a knocking-down iron (see fig. 51), first from the front and then from the back, care being taken that the hammer face should fall squarely, or the slips may be cut. This should rivet them into the board, leaving little or no projection. If in lacing in the fibres should get twisted, no amount of hammering will make them flat, so that it is important in pointing the ends for lacing in, that only the points are twisted just sufficiently

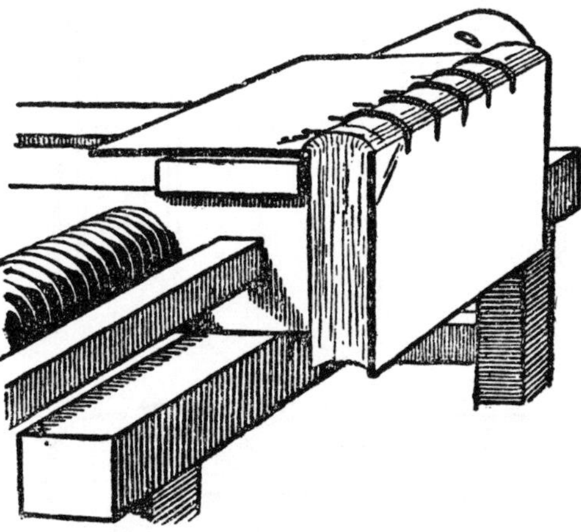

FIG. 51

to facilitate the threading through the holes, and not enough to twist the whole slip.

To lace slips into wooden boards, holes are made with a brace and fine twist bit, and the ends of the frayed out slips may be secured with a wooden plug (see fig. 52).

Old books were sometimes sewn on

bands of leather, but as those sewn on cord seem to have lasted on the whole much better, and as, moreover, modern

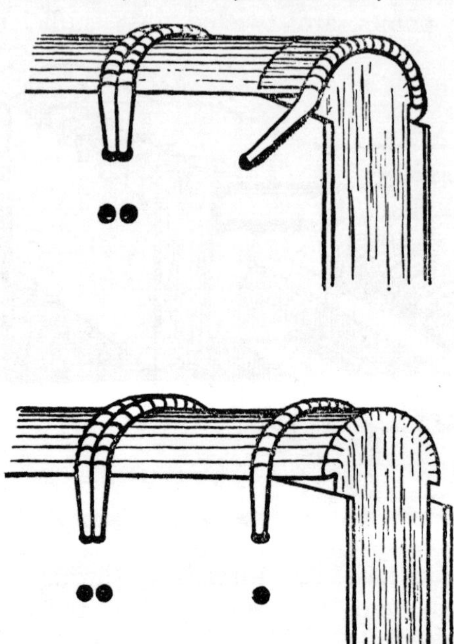

FIG. 52

cord is a far more trustworthy material than modern leather, it is better to use cord for any books bound now.

CLEANING OFF THE BACK AND PRESSING

When the boards have been laced on and the slips hammered down, the book should be pressed. Before pressing, a tin is put on each side of both boards, one being pushed right up into the joint on the inside, and the other up to the joint, or a little over it, on the outside. While in the press, the back should be covered with paste and left to soak for a few minutes. When the glue is soft the surplus on the surface can be scraped off with a piece of wood shaped as shown in fig. 53. For important books it is best to do this in the lying press, but some binders prefer first to build up the books in the standing press, and then to paste the backs and clean them off there. This has the advantage of being a quicker method, and will, in many cases, answer quite well. But for books that require nice adjustment it will be found better to clean off each volume separately in the lying press, and afterwards to build up the books and

Cleaning Off the Back and Pressing

FIG. 53

Cleaning Off the Back and Pressing

boards in the standing press, putting the larger books at the bottom. It must be seen that the entire pile is exactly in the centre under the screw, or the pressure will be uneven. To ascertain if the books are built up truly, the pile must be examined from both the front and side of the press. Each volume must also be looked at carefully to see that it lies evenly, and that the back is not twisted or out of shape. This is important, as any form given to the book when it is pressed at this stage will be permanent.

Any coloured or newly printed plates will need tissues, as in the former pressing; and any folded plates or diagrams or inserted letters will need a thin tin on each side of them to prevent them from marking the book.

Again, the pressure on hand-printed books must not be excessive.

The books should be left in the press at least a night. When taken out they will be ready for head-banding, unless the edges are to be cut in boards.

CHAPTER X

Cutting in Boards—Gilding and Colouring Edges

CUTTING IN BOARDS

Cutting in Boards

THE knife for cutting edges may be ground more acutely than for cutting boards, and should be very sharp, or the paper may be torn. The plough knife should never be ground on the under side, as if the under side is not quite flat, it will tend to run up instead of cutting straight across. Before beginning to cut edges, the position of the knife should be tested carefully by screwing the plough up, with the press a little open, and noting whereabouts on the left-hand cheek the point of the knife comes. In a press that is true the knife should just clear the edge of the press. If there is too much packing the knife will cut below the edge of the press, and if too little, it will cut above.

"Packing" is paper inserted between the knife and the metal plate on the plough, to correct the position of the knife. When by experiment the exact thickness of paper necessary for any given

Cutting in Boards

knife is found, the packing should be carefully kept when the knife is taken out for grinding, and put back with it into the plough.

The first edge to be cut is the top, and the first thing to do is to place the boards in the position they will hold when the book is bound. The front board is then dropped the depth of the square required, care being taken that the back edge of the board remains evenly in the joint. A piece of cardboard, or two or three thicknesses of paper, are then slipped in between the end paper and the back board to prevent the latter from being cut by the knife. The book is then carefully lowered into the press, with the back towards the workman, until the top edge of the front board is exactly even with the right-hand cheek, and the press screwed up evenly. The back board should show the depth of the square above the left-hand cheek. It is very important that the edge of the back board should be exactly parallel with the press, and if at first it is not so, the book must be twisted until it is right.

The edges can now be cut with the plough as in cutting mill-boards. The tail of the book is cut in the same way,

Cutting in Boards

still keeping the back of the book towards the workman, but cutting from the back board.

Cutting the fore-edge is more difficult. The waste sheets at each end of the book should be cut off flush with the edge of the board, and marks made on them below the edge showing the amount of the square, and consequently how much is to be cut off. The curve of the back, and consequent curve of the fore-edge, must first be got rid of, by inserting a pair of pieces of flat steel called "trindles" (fig. 54) across the back, from the inside of the boards. When these are inserted the back must be knocked quite flat, and, in the case of a heavy book, a piece of tape may be tied around the leaves (see fig. 55) to keep them in position. A pair of cutting boards are placed one on each side of the leaves, the back one exactly up to the point that the edge of the board came to, and the front one as much below that point as it is desired the square of the fore-edge should

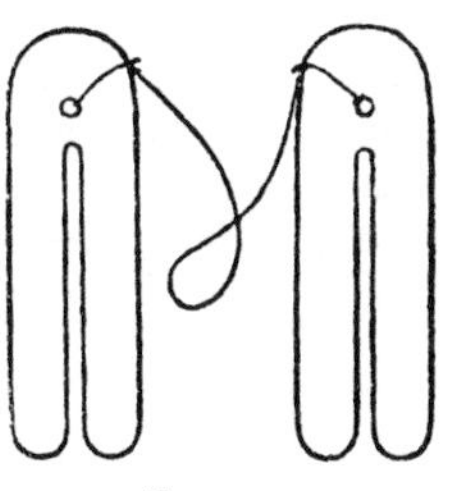
FIG. 54

Cutting in Boards

be. The trindles are removed while the book is held firmly between the cutting boards by the finger and thumb; book and boards are then lowered very carefully into the press. The top edge of the front cutting board should be flush with the right-hand cheek of the press, and that of the back a square above the left-hand cheek (see fig. 56). A further test is to look along the surface of the right-hand cheek, when, if the book has been inserted truly, the amount of the back cutting board in sight should exactly correspond with the amount of the paper to be cut showing above the front board.

Fig. 55

It will also be necessary before cutting to look at the back, and to see that it has remained flat. If it has gone back to its old curve, or the book has been put into the press crookedly, it must be taken right out again and the trindles inserted afresh, it being a waste of time to try to adjust the book in the press. The actual cutting is the same as for the

Cutting in Boards

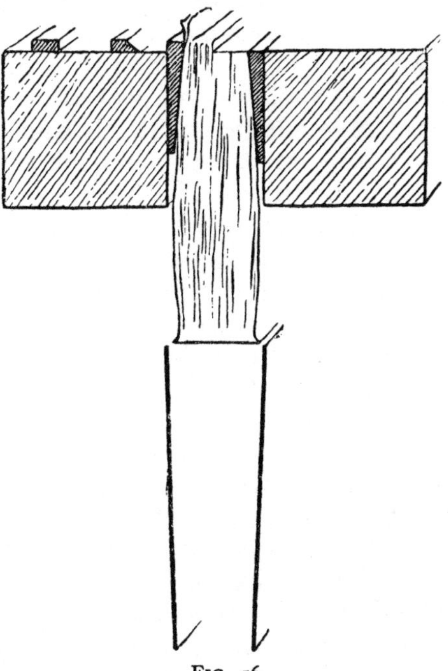

FIG. 56

head and tail. A steady downward pressure must be kept on the plough, and the knife advanced very slightly after each cut.

GILDING OR COLOURING THE EDGES OF A CUT BOOK

Gilding or Colouring the Edges of a Cut Book

Gilding the edges of a book cut in boards is much the same process as that described for the trimmed book, excepting that when gilt in boards the edges can be scraped and slightly sand-papered. It is the custom to admire a perfectly solid gilt edge, looking more like a solid sheet of metal than the leaves of a book. As the essential characteristic of a book is that it is composed of leaves, this fact is better accepted and emphasised by leaving the edges a little rough, so that even when gilt they are evidently the edges of leaves of paper, and not the sides of a block, or of something solid.

To gild the edges of a cut book the boards should be turned back, and cutting boards put on each side of the book flush with the edge to be gilt. For the fore-edge the book must be thrown up with trindles first, unless it is desired to gild in the round, a process which gives the objectionable solid metallic edge.

After the edges have been gilt they may be decorated by tooling, called

Gilding or Colouring the Edges of a Cut Book

"gauffering." This may be done, either by tooling with hot tools directly on the gold while the leaves are screwed up tightly in the press, or by laying another coloured gold on the top of the first and tooling over that, leaving the pattern in the new gold on the original colour. But, to my mind, edges are best left undecorated, except for plain gold or colour.

If the edges are to be coloured, they should be slightly scraped, and the colour put on with a sponge, commencing with the fore-edge, which should be slightly fanned out, and held firmly, by placing a pressing-board above it, and pressing with the hand on this. The colour must be put on very thinly, commencing from the centre of the fore-edge and working to either end, and as many coats put on as are necessary to get the depth of colour required. The head and tail are treated in the same way, excepting that they cannot be fanned out, and the colour should be applied from the back to the fore edge. If in the fore-edge an attempt is made to colour from one end to the other, and if in the head or tail from the fore-edge to the back, the result will almost certainly be that the sponge will leave a thick

Gilding or Colouring the Edges of a Cut Book

deposit of colour round the corner from which it starts.

For colouring edges almost any stain will answer, or ordinary water-colours may be used if moistened with size.

When the colour is dry the edge should be lightly rubbed over with a little beeswax, and burnished with a tooth burnisher (see fig. 57).

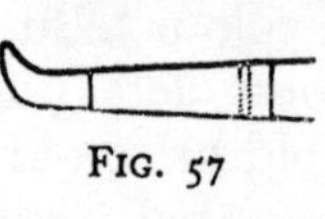

FIG. 57

In addition to plain colour and gilding, the edges of a book may be decorated in a variety of ways. The fore-edge may be fanned out and painted in any device in water-colour and afterwards gilded; the painting will only show when the book is open. The fore-edge for this must be cut quite solid, and if the paper is at all absorbent, must be sized with vellum size before being painted. The paints used must be simple water-colour, and the edge must not be touched with the hand before gilding, as if there is any grease or finger-mark on it, the gold will not stick evenly. Painting on the fore-edge should only be attempted when the paper of the book is thin and of good quality. More common methods of decorating edges are by marbling and sprinkling, but they are both inferior to plain colouring. Some pleasant effects are sometimes obtained by marbling edges and then gilding over the marbling.

Gilding or Colouring the Edges of a Cut Book

CHAPTER XI

Headbanding

HEADBANDS

Headbands

MODERN headbands are small pieces of vellum, gut, or cord sewn on to the head and tail of a book with silk or thread. They resist the strain on the book when it is taken from the shelf. The vellum slip or cord must be of such a depth that when covered with silk it will be slightly lower than the square of the boards. The cut edge of the vellum always slants, and the slip must be placed in position so that it tilts back rather than forward on the book.

To start, ease the boards slightly on the slips and pull them down with the top edges flush with the top edge of the leaves. If this is not done the silk catches on the projecting edges as the band is worked. Stand the book in a finishing press, fore-edge to the worker, and tilted forward so as to give a good view of the headband as it is worked. The light must come from the left, and well on to the work. A needle threaded with silk is put in at the head of the book, and through the centre of the first section after the end papers, and drawn out at the back below the kettle stitch with about two-thirds of the silk. The needle is again inserted in the same place, and drawn through until a loop of silk is left. The vellum slip is placed in the loop, with the end projecting slightly to the left. It must be held steady by a needle placed vertically behind it, with its point between the leaves of the first section. The needle end of silk is then behind the headband, and the shorter end in front. The needle end is brought over from the back with the right hand, passed into the left hand, and held taut. The short end is picked up with the right hand, brought over the needle end under the vellum, and pulled tight from the back. This is repeated; the back thread is again drawn up and over the band to the front, the needle end crosses it, and is drawn behind under the vellum slip, and so on. The crossing of the threads forms a "bead," which must be watched, and kept as tight as possible, and well down on the leaves of the book. Whenever the vellum or string begins to shift in position, it must be tied down. This is done when the needle end of silk is at the back. A finger of the left hand is placed on the thread of silk at the back, and holds it firmly just below the slip. The needle end is then brought up and over the slip, but instead of crossing it with the front thread, the needle is passed between the leaves and out at the back of the book, below the kettle stitch, and the thread gradually drawn tight, and from under the left-hand finger. The loop so made will hold the band firmly, and the silk can then be brought up and over the slip and crossed in the usual way. The band should be worked as far as the end papers, and should be finished with a double "tie down," after which the front thread is drawn under the slip to the back. Both the ends of silk are then cut off to about half an inch, frayed out, and pasted down as flatly as possible on the back of the book.

The band should be tied down frequently. It is not too much to tie down every third time the needle end of the silk comes to the back. To make good headbands the pull on the silk must be even throughout.

When the ends of the silk are pasted down, the ends of the vellum slip are cut off as near the silk as possible. The correct length of the headband is best judged by pressing the boards together with thumb and finger at the opposite ends of the band, so as to compress the sections into their final compass. If the band then buckles in the least, it is too long and must be shortened.

The mediæval headbands were sewn with the other bands (see fig. 32), and were very strong, as they were tied down at every section. Modern worked headbands, although not so strong, are, if frequently tied down, strong enough to resist any reasonable strain. There are many other ways of headbanding, but if the one described is mastered, the various other patterns will suggest themselves if variety is needed. For very large books a double headband may be worked on two pieces of gut or string—a thick piece with a thin piece in front. The string should first be soaked in thin glue and left to dry. Such a band is worked with a figure of eight stitch. Headbands may also be worked with two or three shades of silk. As vellum is apt to get hard and to break when it is used for headbanding, it is well to paste two pieces together with linen in between, and to cut into strips as required.

Machine-made headbands can be bought by the yard. Such bands are merely glued on, but as they have but little strength, should not be used.

Where leather joints are used, the headbands may be worked on pieces of soft leather sized and screwed up. If the ends are left long and tied in front while the book is being covered, they may be conveniently let into grooves in the boards before the leather joint is pasted down. This method, I think, has little constructive value, but it certainly avoids the rather unfinished look of the cut-off headband.

CHAPTER XII

Preparing for Covering—Paring Leather—Covering —Mitring Corners—Filling-in Boards

PREPARING FOR COVERING

Preparing for Covering

AFTER the headband is worked, a piece of brown or other stout paper should be well glued on at the head and tail, care being taken that it is firmly attached to the back and the headband. When dry, the part projecting above the headband is neatly cut off, and the part on the back well sand-papered, to remove any irregularity caused by the tie-downs attaching the headband. For most books this will be quite sufficient lining up, but very heavy books are best further lined up between the bands with linen, or thin leather. This can be put on by pasting the linen or leather and giving the back a very thin coat of glue.

The only thing now left to do before covering will be to set the squares and to cut off a small piece of the back corner of each board at the head and tail, to make it possible for the boards to open and shut without dragging the head-cap out of place. The form of the little piece to be cut off varies with each individual binder, but I have found for an octavo book that a cut slightly sloping from the inside, cutting off the corner about an eighth of an inch each way, gives the best result (see fig. 58). When the corner has been cut off, the boards should be thrown back, and the slips between the book and the board well pasted. When these have soaked a little, the squares of the boards are set; that is, the boards are fixed so that exactly the same square shows on each board above head and tail. A little larger square is sometimes an advantage at the tail to keep the head-cap well off the shelf, the essential thing being that both head and both tail squares should be the same. In the case of an old book that has not been recut, the edges will often be found to be uneven. In such cases the boards must be made square, and so set that the book stands up straight.

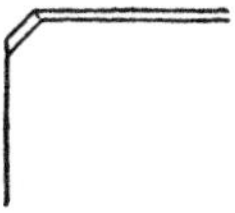

FIG. 58

When the slips have been pasted and the squares set, tins can be put inside and outside the boards, and the book given a

Preparing for Covering

slight nip in the press to flatten the slips. Only a comparatively light pressure should be given, or the lining up of the headbands or back will become cockled and detached.

PARING LEATHER

Paring Leather

While the slips are being set in the press the cover can be got out. Judgment is necessary in cutting out covers. One workman will be able, by careful cutting, to get six covers out of a skin where another will only get four. The firm part of the skin is the back and sides, and this only should be used for the best books. The fleshy parts on the flanks and belly will not wear sufficiently well to be suitable for good bookbinding.

The skin should be cut out, leaving about an inch all round for turning in when the book is covered, and when cut out it must be pared. If the leather is of European manufacture most of the paring will have been done before it is sold, and the leather manufacturer will have shaved it to any thickness required. This is a convenience that is partly responsible for the unduly thin leather that is commonly used. The better plan is to get the leather rather thick, and for the binder to pare it down where necessary. For small books it is essential, in order that the covers may open freely, and the boards not look clumsy, that the leather should be very thin at the joint and round the edges of the boards. For such books it is very important that a small, naturally thin skin should be used that will not have to be unduly pared down, and that the large and thicker skins should be kept for large books.

Paring Leather

Binders like using large skins because there is much less waste, but if these skins are used for small books, so much of the leather substance has to be pared away, that only the comparatively brittle grained surface remains. By the modern process of dyeing this surface is often to some extent injured, and its strength sometimes totally destroyed.

When the cover has been cut to size the book is laid on it with the boards open, and a pencil line drawn round them, a mark being made to show where the back comes. The skin is then pared, making it thin where the edge of the boards will come. Great care must be taken that the thinning does not commence too abruptly, or a ridge will be apparent when the leather is on the book.

The paring must be done quite smoothly and evenly. Every unevenness shows when the cover is polished and pressed. Care is needed in estimating the amount that will have to be pared off that part of the leather that covers the back and joints. The object of the binder should be to leave these portions as thick as he can consistently with the free opening of the boards. The leather at the head-caps must be pared quite thin, as the double thickness on the top of the headband is apt to make this part project above the edges of the board. This is a great trouble, especially at the tail, where, if the head-cap projects beyond the boards, the whole weight of the book rests on it, and it is certain to be rubbed off when the book is put on the shelf.

The method of paring with a French knife (fig. 60, A)—the only form of knife in use by binders that gives sufficient control over the leather—is shown at fig. 59. To use this knife properly, practice is required. The main thing to learn is that the knife must be used quite flat, and made to cut by having a very slight burr

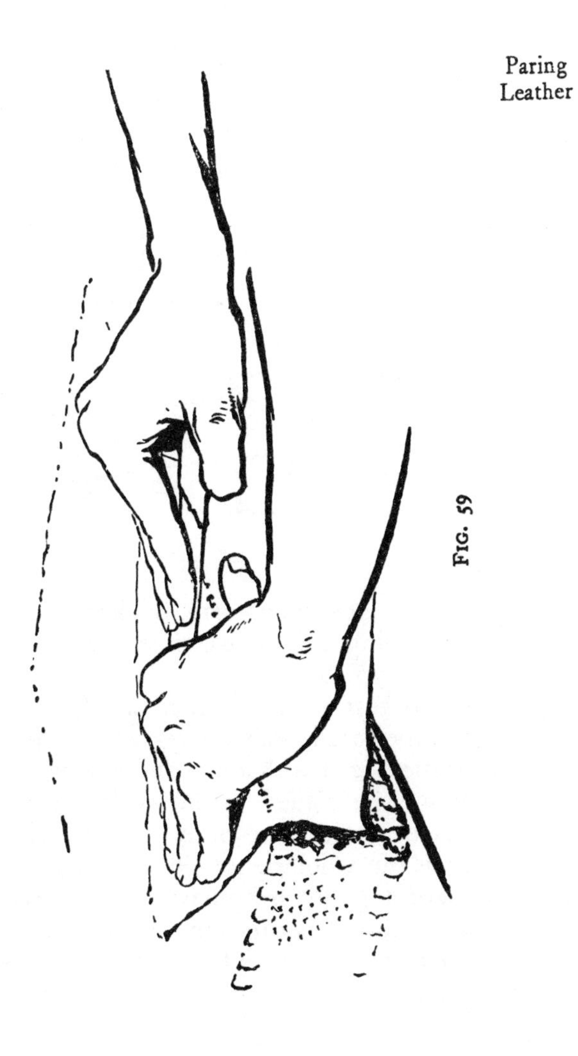

Fig. 59

on the under side. This burr is got by rubbing the knife on the lithographic stone on which the paring is done. The handle of the knife should never be raised to such a height above the surface of the stone that it is possible to get the under fingers of the right hand over the edge of the

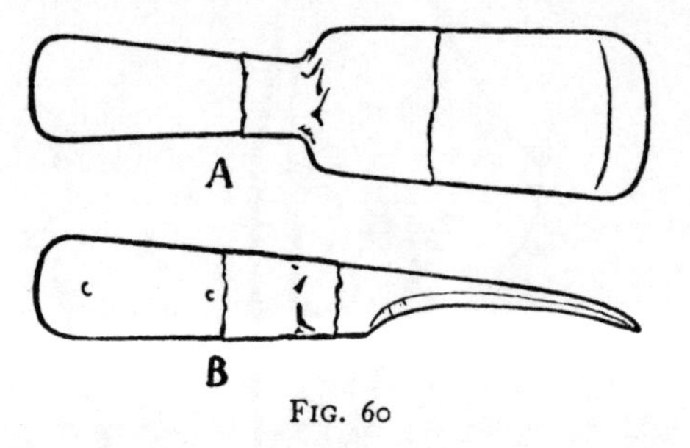

FIG. 60

stone. Another form of knife suitable for paring the edges of leather is shown at fig. 60, B.

To test if the leather has been sufficiently pared, fold it over where the edge of the board will come, and run the finger along the folded leather. If the paring has been done properly it will feel quite even the whole length of the fold; but if there are any irregularities, they will be very apparent, and the paring must be gone over again till they have disappeared.

When even, the book must be again laid on the leather with the boards open, and a pencil line drawn round as before. If there are leather joints they will have been pared before the book was sewn, and care must be taken in paring the turn-in of the cover that it is of the same thickness as the leather joint, or it will be impossible to make a neat mitre at the back corners.

Paring Leather

COVERING

Covering

Before covering, the book must be looked at to see that the bands are quite square and at equal distances apart. Any slight errors in this respect can be corrected by holding the book in the lying press between backing boards and gently tapping the bands from one side or the other with a piece of wood struck with a hammer. This is best done when the back is cleaned off, but by damping the bands slightly it may be done just before covering. The squares must be looked to, and the edges of the board well rubbed with a folder, or tapped with a hammer, to remove any burr that may have been caused by the plough knife, or any chance

Covering

blow. The back is then moistened with paste, or, in the case of a very large book, with thin glue, and left to soak. The cover can then be well pasted with thickish paste, that has been previously well beaten up. When the cover is pasted, it can be folded with the pasted sides together and left to soak for a few minutes

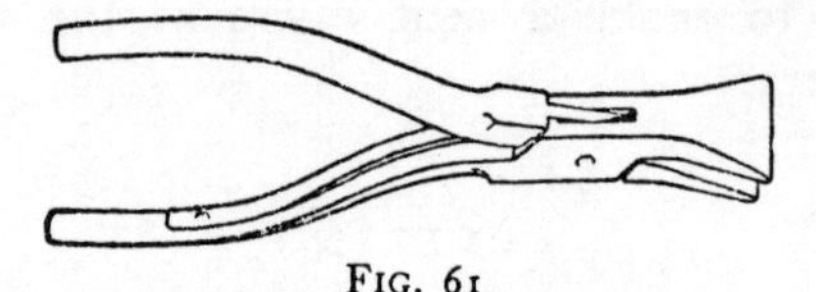

FIG. 61

while the back is again looked to, and any roughness smoothed down with the folder. Before covering, the bands should be nipped up with band nippers (see fig. 61) to make sure that they are sharp. The coverer should have ready before covering a clean paring stone, one or two folders, a pair of nickeled band nippers, a clean sponge, a little water in a saucer, a piece of thread, and a strip of smooth wood (boxwood for preference), called a band stick, used for smoothing the leather between the bands, a pair of scissors, and a small sharp knife, a pair of waterproof sheets the size of the book, and, if the book is a large one, a pair of tying up boards, with tying up string, and two strips of wood covered in blotting-paper or leather. It is best to have the band nippers for covering nickeled to prevent the iron from staining the leather. The waterproof sheets recommended are thin sheets of celluloid, such as are used by photographers.

When these things are ready, the pasted cover should be examined and repasted if it has dried in any place. The amount of paste to be used for covering can only be learned by experience. A thick leather will take more than a thin one, but, provided the cover sticks tight at every point, the less paste used the better. If there is too much, it will rub up and make very ugly, uneven places under the leather; and if there is too little, the cover will not stick.

Take the pasted cover and look to see which is the better side of the leather. Lay the front of the book down on this exactly up to the marks that show the beginning of the turn-in. Then draw the leather over the back and on to the other side, pulling it slightly, but not dragging it. Then stand the book on

Covering its fore-edge on a piece of waste paper, with the leather turned out on either side, as shown in fig. 62, and nip up the bands with nickeled band nippers (see fig. 63).

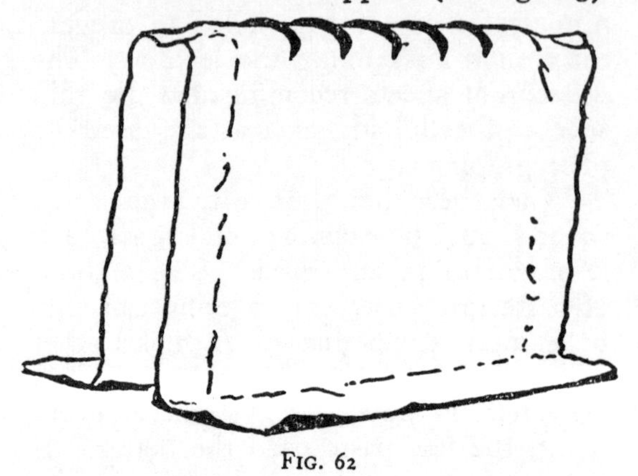

FIG. 62

After this is done there will probably be a good deal of loose leather on the back. This can be got rid of by dragging the leather on to the side; but by far the better plan, when the back is large enough to allow it, is to work up the surplus leather on to the back between the panels. This requires a good deal of practice, and is very seldom done; but it can be done with most satisfactory results. The book should now have the leather on the back stretched lengthways to make it cover the bands, but not stretched the other way, and the leather on the boards should lie perfectly flat and not be stretched at

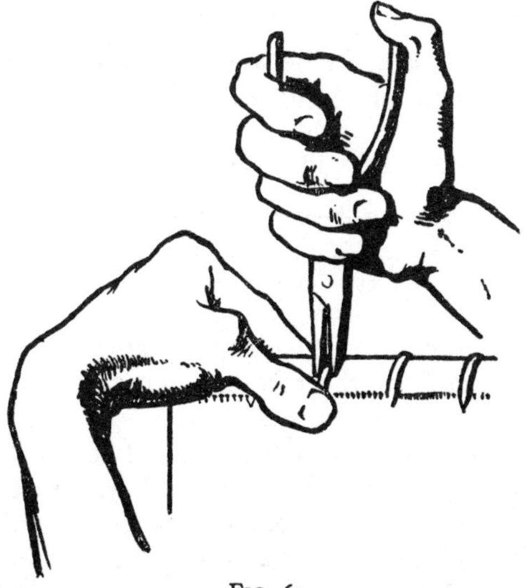

FIG. 63

all. The leather on the fore-edge of the board is then rubbed with the hand on the outside, and then on to the edge, and then on the inside. The edge and the inside are smoothed down with a folder, and any excessive paste on the inside squeezed out and removed. When the fore-edge of both boards has been turned in, the head and tail must also be turned in. A little paste is put on to that part of the leather that will turn in below the headband, and this portion is neatly tucked in between the boards and the back. The turned-in edge must lie quite evenly, or it will result in a ridge on the back. The leather is turned in

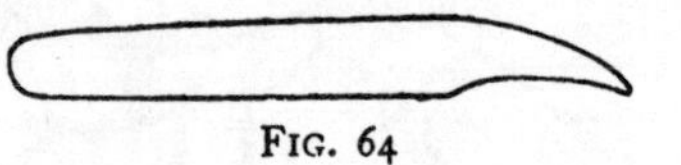

FIG. 64

on the two boards in the same way as described for the fore-edge, and the edge rubbed square with a folder. At fig. 64 is shown a convenient form of folder for covering. At the corners the leather must be pulled over as far as possible with two folders meeting at the extreme point, the object being to avoid a cut in the leather at the corner of the board. The folds so formed must be cut off with the scissors (see fig. 65, A), then one edge tucked neatly under the other (B). Care must be taken throughout not to soil the edges of the leaves.

At the headband the fold of leather,

pared thin for the purpose, must be squeezed together with a folder and pulled out a little to leave an even projection that can be turned over to

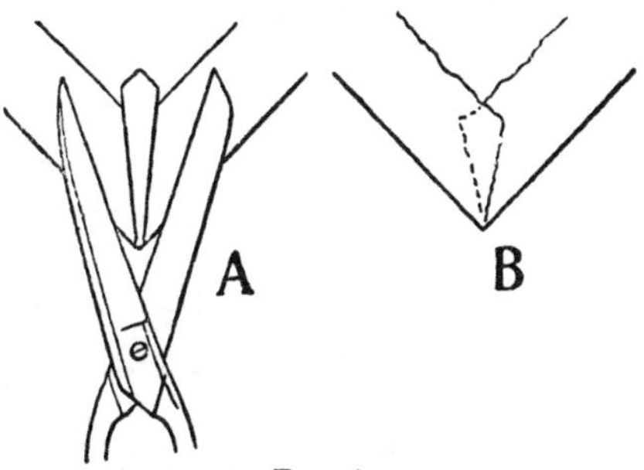

FIG. 65

form a head-cap. When both ends have been turned in, in this way, the boards must each be opened and pressed against a straight-edge held in the joint (fig. 66)

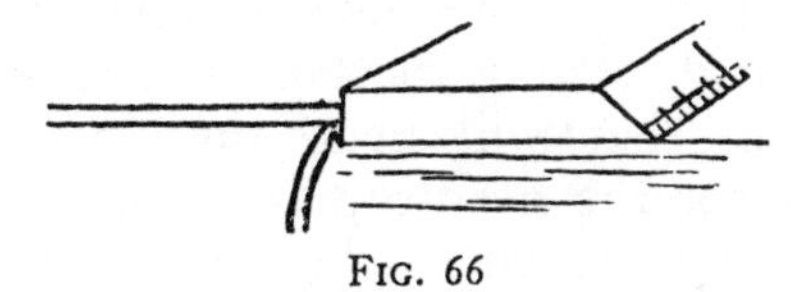

FIG. 66

to ensure that there is enough leather in the turn-in of the joint to allow the cover to open freely; and the leather of the turn-in at the head and tail must be carefully smoothed down with a folder.

The book may now be shut up if a waterproof sheet is put at each end to prevent the damp of the cover from cockling the paper. It must then be stood on its fore-edge and the bands again nipped up with a pair of nickeled band nippers, and the panels between the bands well pressed down with the band stick to cause the leather to stick at every point. A piece of thread is tied round the back from head to tail, squeezing the leather in the gap caused by the corners of the board having been cut off. The book is then turned up on end, resting the tail on a folder or anything that will keep the projecting leather for the head-cap from being prematurely flattened. The head-caps (fig. 67) must now be set. To set a head-cap, the first finger of the left hand is placed behind it, and a sharp folder is pressed into the corners, between the headband and the thread. The leather

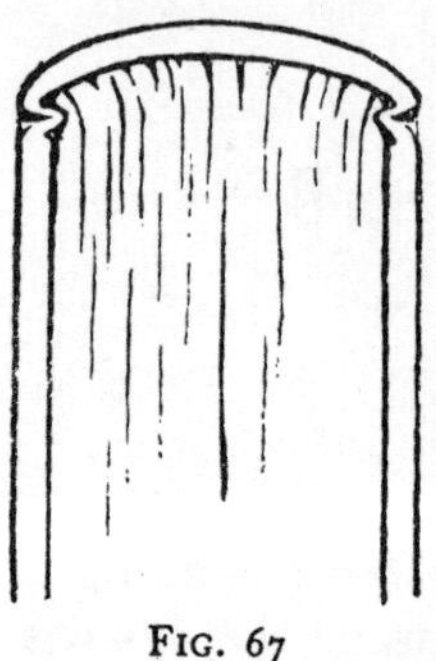

FIG. 67

is then tapped over the headband, and the whole turned over on the stone and rubbed at the back with a folder. This operation requires great nicety. The shape of head-cap is shown at fig. 67. The nice adjustment of head-caps and corners, al-

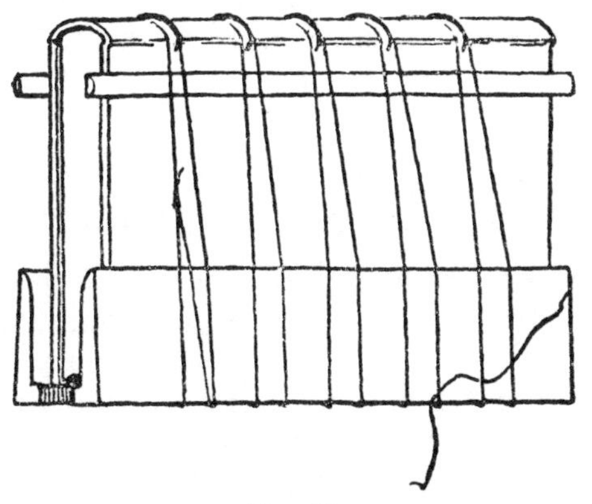

FIG. 68

though of no constructional value, is the point by which the forwarding of a book is generally valued.

If the book is a large one, it will be best to tie it up. The method of tying up is shown in fig. 68. The tying up cords will make marks at the side of the bands that are not unpleasant on a large book. If they are objected to, it is best to tie the book up for about half-an-hour, and then to untie it, and smooth out the marks with the band stick. Even with small books, if the leather seems inclined to give trouble, it is well to tie them up for a short time, then to untie them, to smooth out any marks or inequalities, and to tie them up again.

MITRING CORNERS AND FILLING IN

Mitring Corners and Filling In

A book that has been covered should be left under a light weight until the next day, with waterproof sheets between the damp cover and the end paper to prevent the sheets of the book from cockling through the damp. When the cover is thoroughly set the boards should be carefully opened, pressing them slightly to the joint to ensure a square and even joint. If, as is sometimes the case, the turn-in of the leather over the joint seems to be inclined to bind, the cover should be merely opened half-way, and the leather of the turns-in of the joint damped with a sponge, and left to soak for a short time, and then the cover can usually be opened without any dragging. A section of a good joint is shown at fig. 69, A, and a bad one at B.

Mitring Corners and Filling In

The next operation will be to fill in the board and mitre the corners. To fill in the boards, a piece of paper as thick as

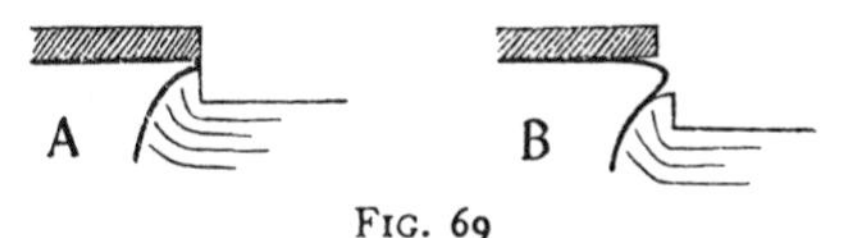

FIG. 69

the turn-in of the leather (engineer's cartridge paper answers very well) should be cut a little smaller than the board, with one edge cut straight; then with the straight edge adjusted to the back of the board, and a weight placed on the centre, the paper is marked round with dividers set to the intended width of the turn-in of the leather. Then with a sharp knife, paper and leather may be cut through together. The paper should then be marked to show its position on the board, and the ragged edges of the leather trimmed off. This will leave an even margin of leather on three sides of the inside of the board, and a piece of paper that will exactly fit the remaining space. The corners must next be mitred.

Mitring Corners and Filling In

To do this, both thicknesses of leather are cut through from the corner of the board to the corner of the inside margin. The knife should be held slightly slanting to make a cut, as shown at fig. 70. The corners should then be thoroughly damped,

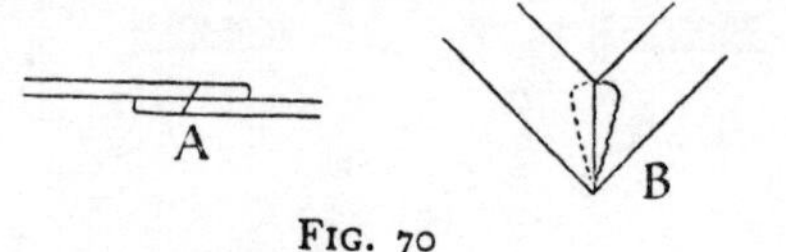

FIG. 70

and the overlapping leather from both sides removed, leaving what should be a neat and straight join. If the leather at the extreme corner should prove to be, as is often the case, too thick to turn in neatly, the corners should be opened out and the leather pared against the thumb nail, and then well pasted and turned back again. The extreme corner may be slightly tapped on the stone with a hammer, and the sides rubbed with a folder, to ensure squareness and sharpness. When all four corners have been mitred, the filling-in papers can be pasted in. As they will probably stretch a little with the paste, it will be well to cut off a slight shaving, and they should then fit exactly. When the boards have been filled in and well rubbed down, the book should be left for some hours with the boards standing open to enable the filling-in papers to draw the boards slightly inwards to overcome the pull of the leather.

Mitring Corners and Filling In

In cases where there are leather joints the operation is as follows: The waste end paper is removed, and the edge of the board and joint carefully cleaned from glue and all irregularities, and if, as is most likely, it is curved from the pull of the leather, the board must be tapped or ironed down until it is perfectly straight. If there is difficulty in making the board lie straight along the joint before pasting down, it will be well first to fill in with a well-pasted and stretched thin paper, which, if the boards are left open, will draw them inwards. If the leather joint is pasted down while the board is curved, the result will be a most unsightly projection on the outside. When the joint has been cleaned out, and the board made to lie flat, the leather should be pasted down and mitred. The whole depth of the turn-in of the covering leather in the joint must not be removed, or it will be unduly weakened. The mitring line should not come from the extreme corner,

Mitring Corners and Filling In

but rather farther down, and there it is well to leave a certain amount of overlap in the joint, for which purpose the edge of the turn-in leather and the edge of the

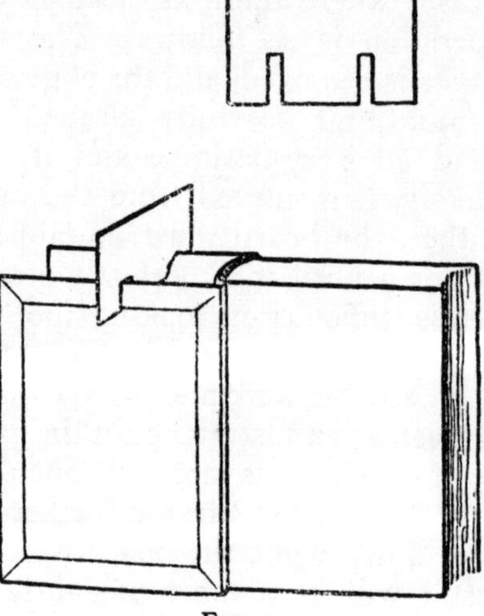

FIG. 71

leather joint should be pared thin. After pasting down the leather joints the boards should be left open till they are dry (see fig. 71). The turn-in and leather joint are then trimmed out, leaving an even margin of leather all round the inside of the board, and the panel in the centre filled in with a piece of thick paper.

Mitring Corners and Filling In

When corners and filling in are dry, the boards may be shut up, and the book is ready for finishing.

It is a common practice to wash up the covers of books that have become stained with a solution of oxalic acid in water. This is a dangerous thing to do, and is likely seriously to injure the leather. Leather, when damp, must not be brought in contact with iron or steel tools, or it may be badly stained.

CHAPTER XIII

Library Binding—Binding Very Thin Books—Scrap-books—Binding in Vellum—Books covered with Embroidery

LIBRARY BINDING

Specifications III and IV

Library Binding

To produce cheaper bindings, as must be done in the case of large libraries, some alteration of design is necessary. Appearance must to some extent be sacrificed to strength and durability, and not, as is too often the case, strength and durability sacrificed to appearance. The essentials of any good binding are that the sections should be sound in themselves, and that there should be no plates or odd sheets "pasted on," or anything that would prevent any leaf from opening right to the back; the sewing must be thoroughly sound; the sewing materials of good quality; the slips firmly attached to the boards; and the leather fairly thick and of a durable kind, although for the sake of cheapness it may be necessary to use skins with flaws on the surface. Such flawed skins cost half, or less than half, the price of perfect skins, and surface flaws do not injure the strength of the leather. By sewing on tape, great flexibility of the back is obtained, and much time, and consequent expense, in covering is saved. By using a French joint much thicker leather than usual can be used, with corresponding gain in strength.

To bind an octavo or smaller book according to the specification given (III, page 309): first make all sections sound, and guard all plates or maps. Make end papers with zigzags. After the sections have been thoroughly pressed, the book will be ready

Library Binding

for marking up and sewing. In marking up for sewing on tapes, two marks will be necessary for each tape. When there are several books of the same size to be sewn, they may be placed one above the other in the sewing press, and sewn on to the same tapes. It will be found that the volumes when sewn can easily be slid along the tapes, which must be long enough to provide sufficient for the slips of each. The split boards may be "made" of a thin black mill-board with a thicker straw-board. To "make" a pair of split boards the pieces of straw- and mill-board large enough to make the two are got out, and the straw-board well glued, except in the centre, which should previously be covered with a strip of thin mill-board or tin about four inches wide. The strip is then removed, and the thin black board laid on the glued straw-board and nipped in the press. When dry, the made board is cut down the centre, which will leave two boards glued together all over except for two inches on one side of each. The boards are then squared to the book in a mill-board machine. The back of the book is glued up, and in the ordinary way rounded and backed. The edges may be cut with a guillotine. The ends of the tapes are glued on the waste end paper, which should be cut off about an inch and a half from the back. The split boards are then opened and glued, and the waste end papers with slips attached are placed in them (see fig. 72), and the book nipped

FIG. 72

in the press. To form a "French joint" the boards should be kept about an eighth of an inch from the back of the book. The book is then ready for covering. The leather must not be pared too thin, as the French joint will give plenty of play and allow the use of much thicker leather than usual. If time and money can be spared, headbands can be worked, but they are not absolutely necessary, and pieces of string may be inserted into the turning of the leather at head and tail in the place of them.

When the book is covered, a piece of string should be tied round the joints, and the whole given a nip in the press. The corners of the boards may be protected by small tips of vellum or parchment. The sides may be covered with cloth or good paper.

Library Binding

The lettering of library books is very important (see Chapter XV).

BINDING VERY THIN BOOKS

Binding very Thin Books

Books consisting of only one section may be bound as follows:—A sheet of paper to match the book, and two coloured sheets for end papers, are folded round the section, and a "waste" paper put over all. A strip of linen is pasted to the back of the waste, and the whole sewn together by stitching through the fold. The waste may be cut off and inserted with the linen in a split board, as for library bindings. The back edges of the board should be filed thin, and should not be placed quite up to the back, to allow for a little play in the joints.

The leather is put on in the ordinary way, except that the linen at the head and

Binding very Thin Books

tail must be slit a little to allow for the turn in. If waterproof sheets are first inserted, the ends may be pasted, the boards shut, and the book nipped in the press. By substituting a piece of thin leather for the outside coloured paper, a leather joint can be made.

SCRAP-BOOKS

Scrap-books

Scrap-books, into which autograph letters, sketches, or other papers can be pasted, may be made as follows:—Enough paper of good quality is folded up to the size desired, and pieces of the same paper, of the same height, and about two inches wide, are folded down the centre and inserted between the backs of the larger sheets, as shown at fig. 73. It is best not to insert these smaller pieces in the centre of the section, as they would be troublesome in sewing. If, after sewing, the book is filled up with waste paper laid between the leaves, it will make it manageable while being forwarded.

It is best to use a rather darkly-toned or coloured paper, as, if a quite white paper is used, any letters or papers that have become soiled will look unduly dirty.

Scrap-books

Autograph letters may be mounted in the following ways:—If the letter is

FIG. 73

written upon both sides of a single leaf, it may be either "inlaid," or guarded, as shown at fig. 74, A. A letter on a folded sheet of notepaper should have the folds strengthened with a guard of strong thin paper, and be attached by a guard made as shown at fig. 74, B; or if on very heavy paper, by a double guard, as shown at

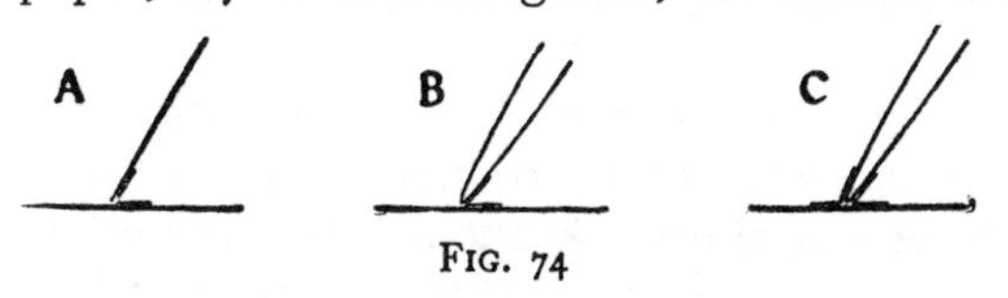

FIG. 74

fig. 74, C. Torn edges of letters may be strengthened with thin Japanese paper.

Thin paper, written or printed only on one side, may be mounted on a page of the book. It is better to attach these by their extreme edges only, as if pasted

Scrap-
books

down all over they may cause the leaves to curl up.

Letters or any writing or drawing in lead pencil should be fixed with size before being inserted.

Silver prints of photographs are best mounted with some very quick-drying paste, such as that sold for the purpose by the photographic dealers. If the leaf on which they are mounted is slightly damped before the photograph is pasted down, it will be less likely to cockle. If this is done, waterproof sheets should be put on each side of the leaf while it dries. If photographs are attached by the edges only, they will not be so liable to draw the paper on which they are mounted; but sometimes they will not lie flat themselves.

In cases where very thick letters or papers have to be pasted in, a few more leaves of the book should be cut out, to make a corresponding thickness of guards at the back.

VELLUM BINDINGS

Vellum
Bindings

Vellum covers may be limp without boards, and merely held in place by the slips being laced through them, or they may be pasted down on boards in much the same way as leather.

If the edges of a book for limp vellum binding are to be trimmed or gilt, that should be done before sewing. For the ends a folded piece of thin vellum may replace the paste-down paper. The sewing should be on strips of vellum. The back is left square after gluing, and headbands are worked as for leather binding, or may be worked on strips of leather, with ends left long enough to lace into the vellum (see p. 151). The back and headbands are lined with leather, and the book is ready for the cover.

A piece of vellum should be cut out large enough to cover the book, and to leave a margin of an inch and a half all round. This is marked with a folder on the under side, as shown at fig. 75, A. Spaces 1 and 2 are the size of the sides of the book with surrounding squares; space 3 is the width of the back, and space 4 the width for the overlaps on the fore-edge. The corners are cut, as shown at 5, and the edges are folded over, as at B. The overlap 4 is then turned over, and the back folded, as at C. The slips are now laced through slits made in the vellum.

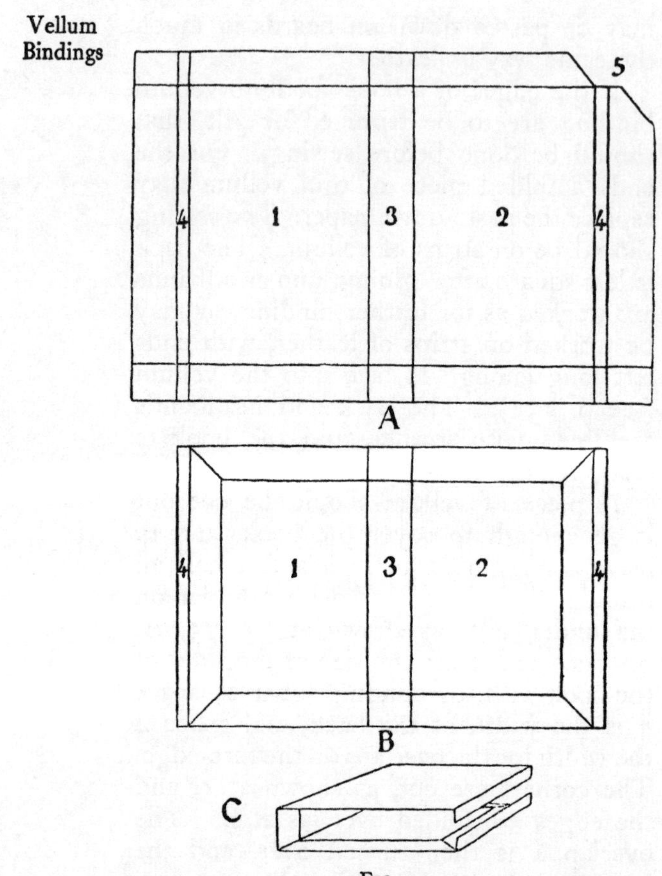

FIG. 75

A piece of loose, toned paper may be put inside the cover to prevent any marks on the book from showing through; and pieces of silk ribbon of good quality are laced in as shown, going through both cover and vellum ends, if there are any, and are left with ends long enough to tie (see fig. 76).

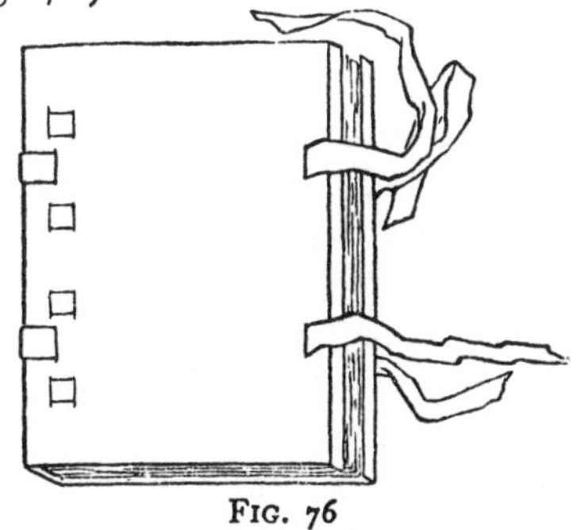

FIG. 76

If paper ends are used, the silk tape need only be laced through the cover, and the end paper pasted over it on the inside.

Another simple way of keeping a vellum book shut is shown at fig. 77. A bead is attached to a piece of gut laced into the vellum, and a loop of catgut is laced in the other side, and looped over the bead as shown.

If the book is to have stiff boards, and

the vellum is to be pasted to them, it is best to sew the sections on tapes or vellum slips, to back the book as for leather, and to insert the ends of the slips in a split board, leaving a French joint, as described for library bindings. Vellum is very stiff, and, if it is pasted directly to the back, the book would be hard to open. It is best in this case to use what is known as a hollow back.

FIG. 77

To make a hollow back, a piece of stout paper is taken which measures once the length of the back and three times the width. This is folded in three. The centre portion is glued to the back and well rubbed down, and the overlapping edges turned back and glued one to the other (fig. 78). This will leave a flat, hollow casing, formed by the single paper glued to the back of the book and the double paper to which the vellum may be attached. Or it is better to line up the back with leather, and to place a piece of thick paper the size of the back on to the pasted vellum where the back will be when the book is covered.

When the book is ready for covering, the vellum should be cut out and lined with paper. In lining vellum the paste must be free from lumps, and great care must be taken not to leave brush marks. To avoid this, when the lining paper has been pasted it can be laid, paste downwards, on a piece of waste paper and quickly pulled up again; this should remove surplus paste and get rid of any marks left by the brush. When the vellum has been lined with paper, it should be given a light nip in the press between blotting-paper, and while still damp it is pasted, the book covered, and the corners mitred. A piece of thin string is tied round the head-caps and pressed into the French joint.

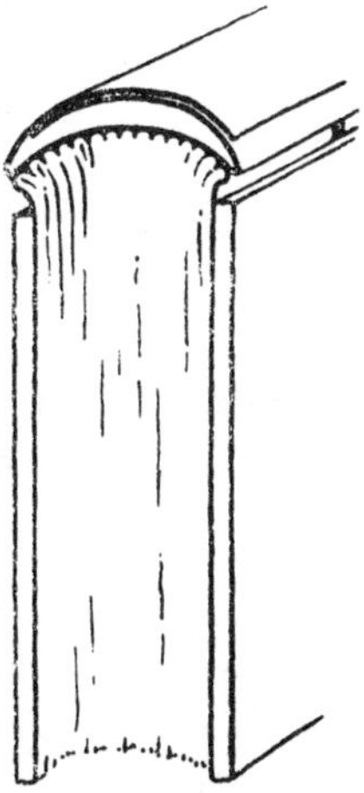

FIG. 78

Waterproof sheets are placed inside the covers, and the book then nipped in the press and left to dry under a light weight. If the vellum is very stiff and difficult to turn in, it may be moistened with a little warm water to soften it.

Books with raised bands have sometimes been covered with vellum, but the back

Vellum Bindings

becomes so stiff and hard, that this method, though it looks well enough, cannot be recommended. Vellum is a durable material, and can be had of good quality, but it is so easily influenced by changes of temperature that it is rather an unsuitable material for most bindings.

BOOKS COVERED WITH EMBROIDERY AND WOVEN MATERIAL

Books Covered with Embroidery and Woven Material

To cover a book with embroidered material bind it with split boards, a French joint, and a hollow back, as described for vellum (see fig. 78). Glue the back of the book with thin glue well worked up, and turning in the head and tail of the embroidery, put the book down on it so that the back will come exactly in the right place. Press down the embroidery with the hand to make sure that it sticks. When it is firmly attached to the back, first one board and then the other should be glued, and the embroidery laid down on it. Lastly, the edges are glued and stuck down on the inside of the board, and the corners mitred. Velvet or any other thick material can be put down in the same way. For very thin material that the glue would penetrate and soil, the cover should be left loose, and only attached where it turns in. A loose lining of good paper may be put between the book and the cover.

Books Covered with Embroidery and Woven Material

The inside corners where the cover has been cut should be neatly sewn up. The edges of the boards and head-caps may be protected all round with some edging worked in metal thread. It is well in embroidering book covers to arrange for some portion of the pattern to be of raised metal stitches, forming bosses that will protect the surface from wear.

Should any glue chance to get on the surface, the cover should be held in the steam of a kettle and the glue wiped off, and the cover again steamed.

CHAPTER XIV

Decoration—Tools—Finishing—Tooling on Vellum—Inlaying on Leather

DECORATION OF BINDING—TOOLS

Decoration of Binding —Tools

THE most usual, and perhaps the most characteristic, way of decorating book covers is by "tooling." Tooling is the impression of heated (finishing) tools. Finishing tools are stamps of metal that

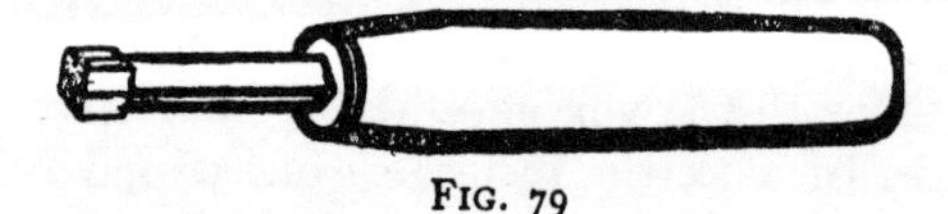

FIG. 79

have a device cut on the face, and are held in wooden handles (fig. 79).

Tooling may either be blind tooling, that is, a simple impression of the hot tools, or gold tooling, in which the impression of the tool is left in gold on the leather.

Tools for blind tooling are best "die-sunk," that is, cut like a seal. The "sunk" part of the face of the tool, which may be more or less modelled, forms the pattern, and the higher part depresses the leather to form a ground. In tools for gold tooling, the surface of the tool gives the pattern.

Tools may be either complex or simple in design, that is to say, each tool may form a complete design with enclosing border, as the lower ones on page 323, or it may be only one element of a design, as at fig. 100. Lines may be run with a fillet (see fig. 88), or made with gouges or pallets.

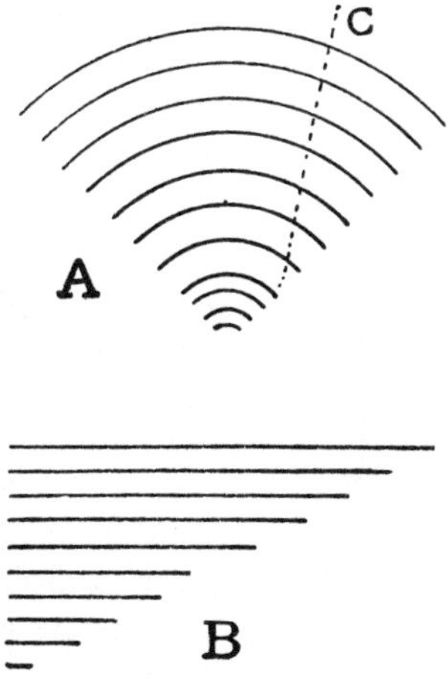

Gouges are curved line tools. They are made in sets of arcs of concentric circles (see fig. 80, A). The portion of the curves cut off by the dotted line C will make a second set with flatter curves. Gouges are used for tooling curved lines.

C

A

B

FIG. 80

A "pallet" may be described as a segment of a roll or fillet set in a handle, and used chiefly for putting lines or other ornaments across the backs of books (see fig. 81). Set of one line pallets shown at fig. 80, B.

Fillets are cut with two or more lines on the edge. Although the use of double-line fillets saves time, I have found that a few single-line fillets with edges of different gauges are sufficient for running all straight lines, and that the advantage of being able to alter the distances between any parallel lines is ample compensation for the extra trouble involved by their use. In addition to the rigid stamps, an endless pattern for either blind or gold tooling may be engraved on the circumference of a roll, and impressed on the leather by wheeling.

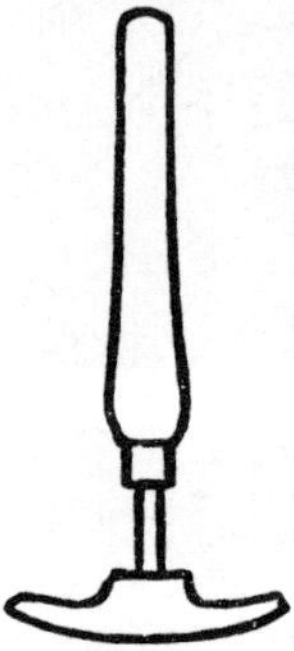

Fig. 81

The use of a roll in finishing dates from the end of the fifteenth century, and some satisfactory bindings were decorated with its aid. The ease with which it can be used has led in modern times to its abuse, and I hardly know of a single instance of a modern binding on which rolls have been used for the decoration with satisfactory results. The gain in time and trouble is at the expense of freedom and life in the design; and for extra binding it is better to build up a pattern out of small tools of simple design, which can be arranged in endless variety, than to use rolls.

Decoration of Binding —Tools

Tools for hand-tooling must not be too large, or it will be impossible to obtain clear impressions. One inch square for blind tools, or three-quarters of an inch for gold tools, is about the maximum size for use with any certainty and comfort. Tools much larger than this have to be worked with the aid of a press, and are called blocks.

FINISHING

Finishing

The first thing the finisher does to a book is to go over the back with a polisher and smooth out any irregularities.

Two forms of polisher are shown at fig. 82. The lower one is suitable for polishing backs and inside margins, and the upper for sides. Polishers must be used warm, but not too hot, or the leather may be scorched, and they must be kept moving on the leather. Before using they should be rubbed bright on a piece of the finest emery-paper, and polished on a piece of leather. New polishers often have sharp edges that would mark the leather. These must be rubbed down with files and emery-paper.

Leathers with a prominent grained surface, such as morocco, seal, or pig skin

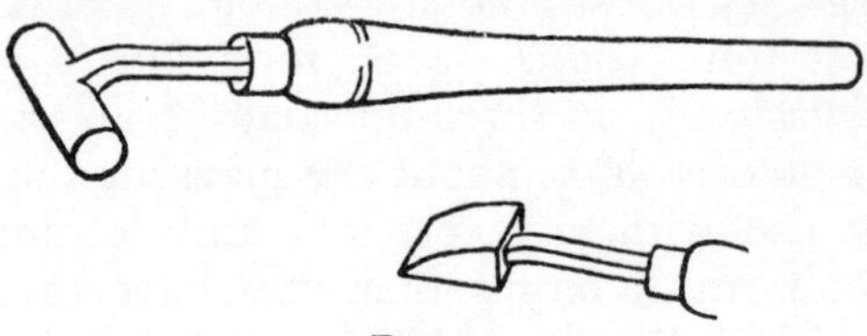

FIG. 82

may have the grain either rough or crushed flat. If there is to be much finishing, the grain had better be crushed, but for large books that are to have only a small amount of finishing, the grain is best left unflattened.

If the grain of the leather is to be "crushed," it may be done at this stage. To do this, one board at a time is damped with a sponge and put in the standing press, with a pressing plate on the grained side, and a pad of blotting-paper, or some such yielding substance, on the other (see fig. 83). The press is then screwed up tight, and the board left for a short time. For some leathers this operation is best done after the binding has been finished and varnished, in which case, of course, the boards cannot be damped before pressing. No flexibly sewn book should be subject to great pressure after it has been covered, or the leather on the back may crinkle up and become detached.

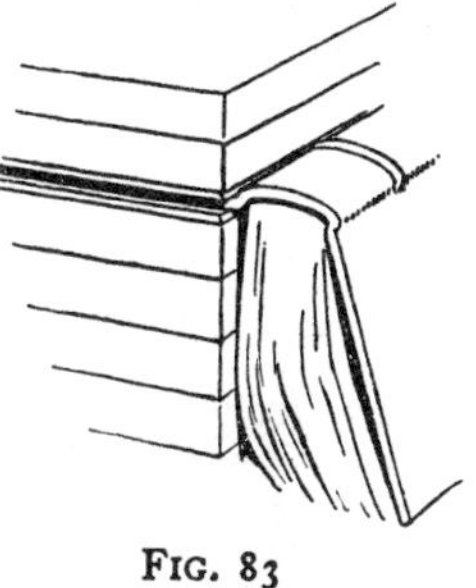
Fig. 83

The next thing will be to decide what lettering and what decoration, if any, is to be put on the volume. The lettering should be made out first (see page 215). If the book is to be at all elaborately decorated, paper patterns must be made out, as described in Chapter XVI.

For tooling the back, the book is held in the finishing press between a pair of backing boards lined with leather (see fig. 84), and the paper pattern put across the back, with the ends either slightly pasted to the backing boards, or caught between them and the book.

For the sides, the pattern is very slightly pasted on to the leather at the four corners. The book is then put in the finishing press, with the board to be tooled open and flat on the cheek of the press, unless the book is a large one, when it is easier to tool the sides out of the press.

The selected tools, which should be ready on the stove (see fig. 85), are one at a time cooled on a wet pad, and then

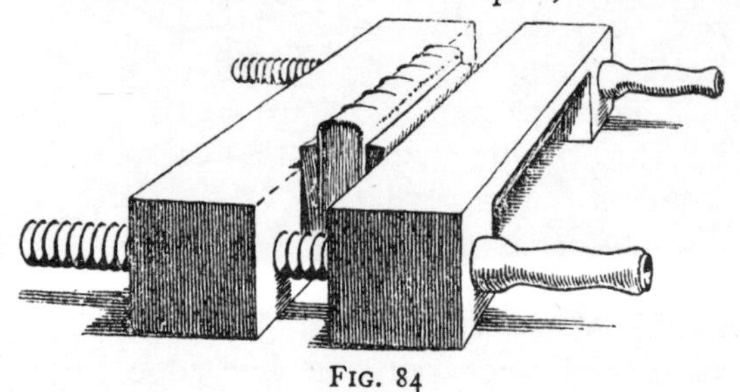

FIG. 84

pressed in their former impressions upon the paper. The degree of heat required varies a good deal with the leather used, and will only be learned by experience. It is better to have the tool too cool than too hot, as it is easy to deepen impressions after the paper is removed; but if they are already too deep, or are burnt, it will be impossible to finish clearly. Generally speaking, tools should hiss very slightly when put on the cooling pad. In cooling,

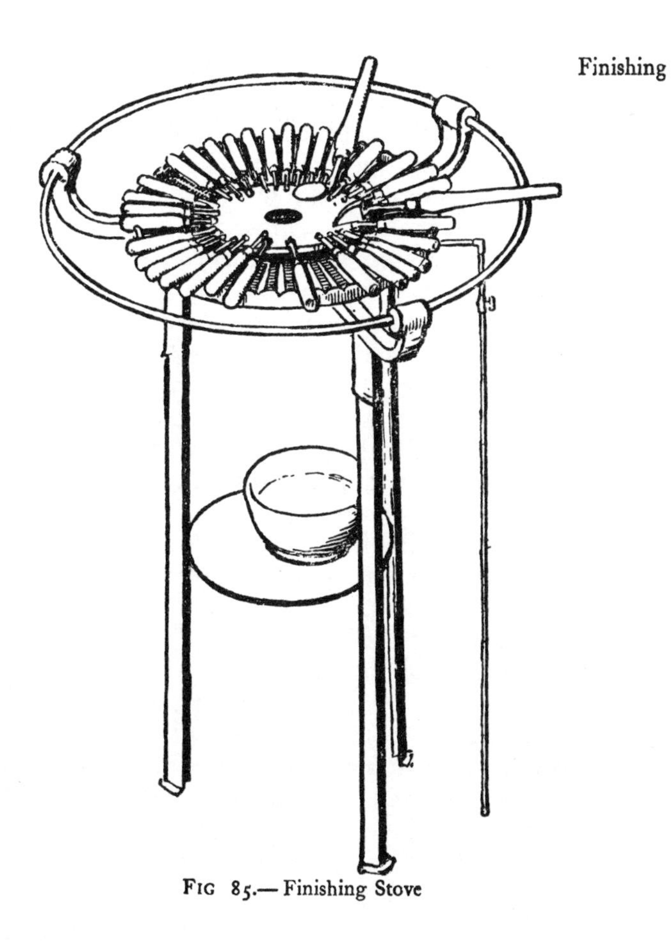

FIG 85.—Finishing Stove

care must be taken to put the shank of the tools on to the wet pad, as, if the end only is cooled, the heat is apt to run down again, and the tool will still be too hot.

Before removing the paper, one corner at a time should be lifted up, and the leather examined to see that no part of the pattern has been missed.

In some patterns where the design is close, or in which the background is dotted in, it will not be necessary to blind in every leaf and dot through the paper. If the lines with perhaps the terminal leaves are blinded in, the rest can be better worked directly through the gold. This method implies the "glairing in" of the whole surface. It is not suitable for open patterns, where the glaire might show on the surface of the leather.

If the book is only to have lines, or some simple straight line pattern, it is often easier to mark it up without the paper, with a straight-edge and folder. In panelling a back, the side lines of all the panels should be marked in at the same time with a folder, working against the straight-edge, held firmly at the side of the back. If the panels are worked separately, it is difficult to get the side lines squarely above each other. The lines at the top and bottom of the panel may be marked in with a folder, guided by a piece of stiff vellum held squarely across the back. If there are lines to be run round the board, they can be marked in with a pair of dividers guided by the edge of the board, except those at the back. These must be measured from the fore-edge of the board and run in with straight-edge and folder.

When straight lines occur in patterns that are blinded through the paper, it will be enough if the ends only are marked through with a small piece of straight line, and the lines completed with straight-edge and folder, after the paper has been removed.

Unless the finisher has had considerable experience, it is best to deepen all folder lines by going over them in blind with a fillet or piece of straight line.

When the pattern has been worked in blind, either through a paper pattern or directly on to the leather with the tools, and any inlays stuck on (see page 213), the cover should be well washed with clean water. Some finishers prefer to use common vinegar or diluted acetic acid for washing up books. If vinegar is used it must be of the best quality, and must not contain any sulphuric acid. Cheap, crude vinegar is certain to be injurious to the leather. Porous leather, such as seal, calf, or sheep skin, will need to be washed over with paste-water, and then sized.

Paste-water is paste and water well beaten up to form a milky liquid, and is applied to the leather as evenly as possible with a sponge. When the paste-water is dry, the leather should be washed with size. Size can be made by boiling down vellum cuttings, or by dissolving gelatine or isinglass in warm water.

For the less porous leathers, such as morocco or pig skin, no paste-water or size is necessary, unless the skin happens to be a specially open one, or the cover has been cut from the flank or belly. Then it is best to put a little paste in the vinegar or water used for washing up. When the leather is nearly, but not quite, dry the impressions of the tools must be painted with glaire. Finishers' glaire may be made from the white of eggs well beaten up, diluted with about half as much vinegar, and allowed to settle. Some finishers prefer to use old, evil-smelling glaire, but provided it is a day old, and has been well beaten up, fresh glaire will work quite well.

The impressions of any heavy or solid tools should be given a second coat of glaire when the first has ceased to be "tacky," and if the leather is at all porous, all impressions had better have a second coat.

As glaire is apt to show and disfigure the leather when dry, it is best to use it as sparingly as possible, and, excepting where the pattern is very close, to confine it to the impressions of the tools. It is not at all an uncommon thing to see the effect of an otherwise admirably tooled binding spoilt by a dark margin round the tools, caused by the careless use of glaire. Glaire should not be used unless it is quite liquid and clean. Directly it begins to get thick it should be strained or thrown away.

The finisher should not glaire in more than he can tool the same day. When the glaire has ceased to be "tacky," the gold is laid on.

At first it will be found difficult to manage gold leaf. The essential conditions are, that there should be no draught, and that the cushion and knife should be quite free from grease. The gold cushion and knife are shown at fig. 86. A little powdered bath-brick rubbed into the cushion will make it easier to cut the gold cleanly. The blade of the gold knife should never be touched with the hand, and before using it, both sides should be rubbed on the cushion. A book of gold

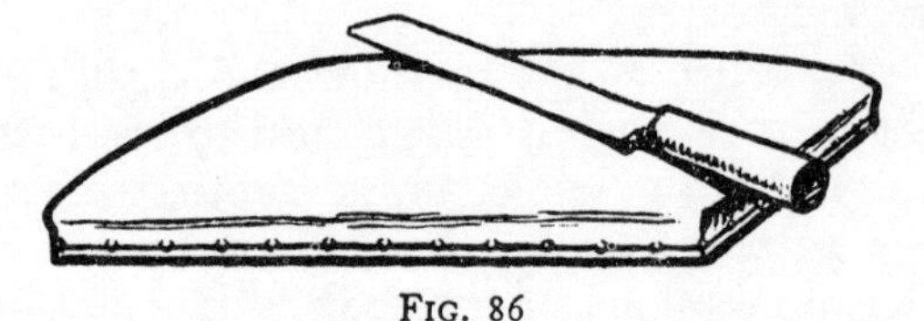

Fig. 86

is laid open on the cushion, and a leaf of gold is lifted up on the gold knife, which is slipped under it, and turned over on to the cushion. A light breath exactly in the centre of the leaf should make it lie flat, when it may be cut into pieces of any size with a slightly sawing motion of the knife. The book with the pattern ready prepared, and the glaire sufficiently dry (not sticky), is rubbed lightly with a small piece of cotton-wool greased with a little coco-nut oil. The back of the hand is greased in the same way, and a pad of clean cotton-wool is held in the right hand, and having been made as flat as possible by being pressed on the table, is drawn over the back of the hand. This should make it just greasy enough to pick up the gold, but not too greasy to part with it readily when pressed on the book. As little grease as possible should be used on the book, as an excess is apt to stain the leather and to

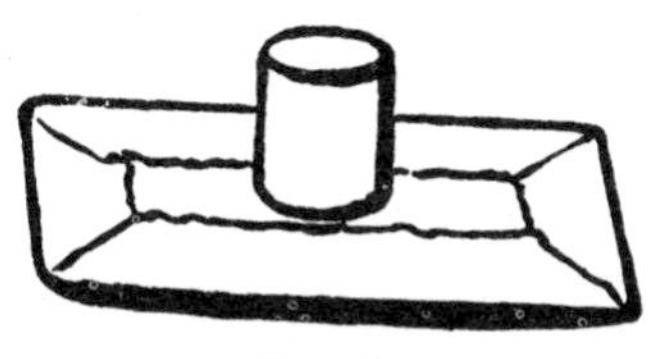

FIG. 87

make the gold dull. After experiment it has been found that coco-nut oil stains the leather less than any other grease in common use by bookbinders, and is more readily washed out by benzine.

If the gold cracks, or is not solid when pressed on the book, a second thickness should be used. This will stay down if the under piece is lightly breathed upon.

For narrow strips of gold for lines, a little pad covered with soft leather may be made, as in fig. 87.

It will be found of advantage first to use the bottom leaf of gold in the book and then to begin at the top and work through, or else the bottom leaf will almost certainly be found to be damaged by the time it is reached. The gold used should be as nearly pure as it can be got. The gold-beaters say that they are unable to beat pure gold as thin as is usual for gold leaf; but the quite pure gold is a better colour than when alloyed, and the additional thickness, although costly, results in a more solid impression of the tools.

The cost in 1901 of a book of twenty-five leaves three and a quarter inches square of English gold leaf of good ordinary quality was from 1s. 3d. to 1s. 6d., whereas the cost of a book of double thick pure gold leaf was 3s. to 3s. 6d. For tooled work it is worth paying the increased price for the sake of the advantages in colour and solidity; but for lines and edges, which use up an immense amount of gold, the thinner and cheaper gold may quite well be used.

Besides pure gold leaf, gold alloyed with various metals to change its colour can be had. None of the alloys keeps its colour as well as pure gold, and some of them, such as those alloyed with copper for red gold, and with silver for pale gold, tarnish very quickly. These last are not to be recommended.

For silver tooling aluminium leaf may be used, as silver leaf tarnishes very quickly.

When the gold is pressed into the impressions of the tools with the pad of cotton-wool, they should be plainly visible through it.

The pattern must now be worked through the gold with the hot tools. The tools are taken from the stove, and if too hot cooled on a pad as for blinding-in. The heat required to leave the gold tooling solid and bright and the impressions clear will vary for different leathers, and even for different skins of the same leather. For trial, a tool may be laid on the pad until it ceases to hiss, and one or two impressions worked with it. If the gold fails to stick, the heat may be slightly increased.

If the leather is slightly damp from the preparation the tools will usually work better, and less heat is required than if it has been prepared for some time and has got dry.

Before using, the faces of all tools must be rubbed bright on the flesh side of a piece of leather. It is impossible to tool brightly with dirty tools. A tool should be held in the right hand, with the thumb on the top of the handle, and steadied with the thumb or first finger of the left hand. The shoulder should be brought well over the tool, and the upper part of the body used as a press. If the weight of the body is used in finishing, the tools can be worked with far greater firmness and certainty, and with less fatigue, than if the whole work is done with the muscles of the arms.

Large and solid tools will require all the weight that can be put on them, and even then the gold will often fail to stick with one impression. Tools with small surfaces, such as gouges and dots, must not be worked too heavily, or the surface of the leather may be cut.

To strike a large or solid tool, it should first be put down flat, and then slightly rocked from side to side and from top to bottom, but must not be twisted on the gold.

A tool may be struck from whichever side the best "sight" can be got, and press and book turned round to the most convenient position.

It is difficult to impress some tools,

such as circular flower tools, twice in exactly the same place. Such tools should have a mark on one side as a guide. This should always be kept in the same position when blinding-in and tooling, and so make it possible to impress a second time without "doubling." An impression is said to be "doubled" when the tool has been twisted in striking, or one impression does not fall exactly over the other.

The hot tool should not be held hovering over the impression long, or the preparation will be dried up before the tool is struck. Tooling will generally be brighter if the tools are struck fairly sharply, and at once removed from the leather, than if they are kept down a long time.

To "strike" dots, the book should be turned with the head to the worker, and the tool held with the handle inclining slightly towards him. This will make them appear bright when the book is held the right way up.

Gouges must be "sighted" from the inside of the curve, and struck evenly, or the points may cut into the leather. Short straight lines may be put in with pieces of line, and longer ones with a fillet.

A one line fillet is shown at fig. 88; the space filed out of the circumference is to enable lines to be joined neatly at the corners. That the lines may be clearly visible through the gold, the book should be placed so that the light comes from the left hand of the worker and across the

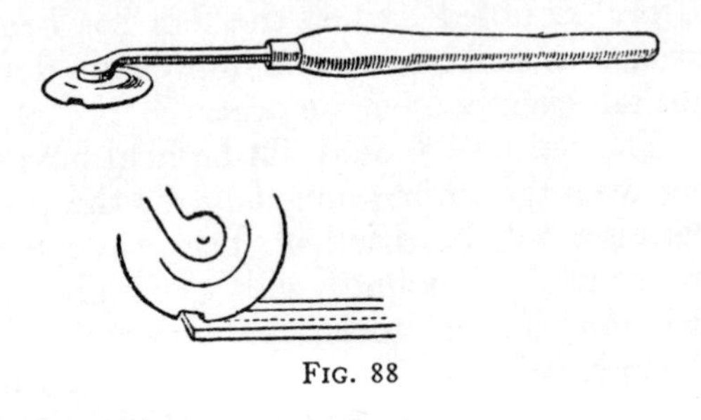

FIG. 88

line. It is well to have a basin of water in which to cool fillets, as there is so much metal in them that the damp sponge or cotton used for cooling tools would very rapidly be dried up. When the fillet has been cooled, the edge should be rubbed on the cleaning pad, and the point exactly adjusted to the corner of the line to be run (see fig. 88). The fillet is then run along the line with even pressure.

For slightly curved lines, a very small fillet may be used.

When all the prepared part of a pattern has been tooled, it is well rubbed to remove the loose gold with a slightly greasy rag, or with a piece of bottle indiarubber which has been softened in paraffin. After a time the rubber or rag may be sold to the gold-beater, who recovers the gold. To prepare indiarubber for cleaning off gold, a piece of bottle rubber is cut into small pieces and soaked in paraffin for some hours. This should cause the pieces to reunite into a soft lump. This can be used until it is yellow with gold throughout.

When all free gold is rubbed off, the finisher can see where the tooling is imperfect. Impressions which are not "solid" must be reglaired, have fresh gold laid on, and be retooled. But if, as will sometimes happen with the best finishers, the gold has failed to stick properly anywhere, it is best to wash the whole with water or vinegar, and prepare afresh.

As an excess of grease is apt to dull the gold and soil the leather, it is better to use it very sparingly when laying on fresh gold for mending. For patching, benzine may be used instead of grease. When the gold is picked up on the cotton-wool pad, rapidly go over the leather with wool soaked in benzine, and at once lay down the gold. Benzine will not hold the gold long enough for much tooling, but it will answer for about half-a-minute, and give plenty of time for patching.

Imperfect tooling arises from a variety of causes. If an impression is clear, but the gold not solid, it is probably because the tool was not hot enough, or was not put down firmly. If only one side of an impression fails to stick, it is usually because the tool was unevenly impressed. If an impression is blurred, and the gold has a frosted look, it is because the leather has been burned, either because the tool was too hot, or kept down too long, or the preparation was too fresh.

To mend double or burnt impressions the leather should be wetted and left to soak a short time, and the gold can be picked out with a wooden point. When nearly dry the impressions should be put in again with a cool tool, reglaired and retooled.

It is very difficult to mend neatly if the leather is badly burned. Sometimes it may be advisable to paste a piece of new leather over a burnt impression before retooling.

If a tool is put down in the wrong

place by mistake, it is difficult to get the impression out entirely. The best thing to do is to damp the leather thoroughly, leave it to soak for a little while, and pick up the impression with the point of a pin. It is best not to use an iron point for this, as iron is apt to blacken the leather.

Leather is difficult to tool if it has not a firm surface, or if it is too thin to give a little when the tool is struck.

When the tooling is finished, and the loose gold removed with the rubber, the leather should be washed with benzine, to remove any grease and any fragments of gold that may be adhering by the grease only.

The inside margins of the boards are next polished and varnished, and the end papers pasted down. Or if there is a leather joint, the panel left on the board may be filled in (see Chapter XVII).

When the end papers are dry, the sides and back may be polished and varnished.

It is important that the varnish should be of good quality, and not too thick, or it will in time turn brown and cause the gold to look dirty. Some of the light French spirit varnishes prepared for bookbinders answer well. Varnish must be used sparingly, and is best applied with a pad of cotton-wool. A little varnish is poured on to the pad, which is rubbed on a piece of paper until it is seen that the varnish comes out thinly and evenly. It is then rubbed on the book with a spiral motion. The quicker the surface is gone over, provided every part is covered, the better. Varnish will not work well if it is very cold, and in cold weather both the book and varnish bottle should be slightly warmed before use. Should an excess of varnish be put on in error, or should it be necessary to retool part of the book after it has been varnished, the varnish can be removed with spirits of wine. Varnish acts as a preservative to the leather, but has the disadvantage, if used in excess, of making it rather brittle on the surface. It must, therefore, be used very sparingly at the joints. It is to be hoped that a perfectly elastic varnish, that will not tarnish the gold, will soon be discovered.

As soon as the varnish is dry the boards may be pressed, one at a time, to give the leather a smooth surface (see fig. 83), leaving each board in the press for some hours.

After each board has been pressed separately, the book should be shut, and pressed

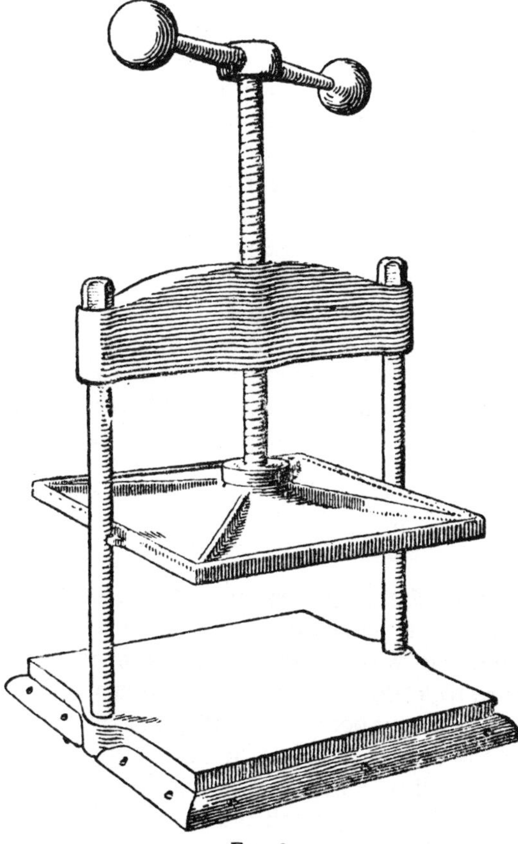

FIG. 89

Finishing again with pressing plates on each side of it, and with tins covered with paper placed inside each board. Light pressure should be given to books with tight backs, or the leather may become detached.

If, on removing from the press, the boards will not keep shut, the book should be pressed again with a folded sheet of blotting-paper in each end. The blotting-paper should have the folded edge turned up, and be placed so that this turned-up edge will be in the joint behind the back edge of the board when the book is shut.

A small nipping-press, suitable for giving comparatively light pressure, is shown at fig. 89.

TOOLING ON VELLUM

Tooling on Vellum

Most covering vellum has a sticky surface, that marks if it is handled. This should be washed off with clean water before tooling. The pattern is blinded in through the paper as for leather, excepting that the paper must not be pasted directly to the vellum, but may be held with a band going right round the board or book. It is best to glaire twice, and to lay on a small portion of gold at a time with benzine. As vellum burns very readily, the tools must not be too hot, and some skill is needed to prevent them from slipping on the hard surface.

Tooling on Vellum

Vellum must not be polished or varnished.

INLAYING ON LEATHER

Inlaying on Leather

Inlaying or onlaying is adding a different leather from that of the cover, as decoration. Thus on a red book, a panel or a border, or other portion, may be covered with thin green leather, or only flowers or leaves may be inlaid, while a jewel-like effect may be obtained by dots, leaves, and flowers, tooled over inlays of various colours. Leather for inlaying should be pared very thin. To do this the leather is cut into strips, wetted, and pared on a stone with a knife shaped somewhat as at fig. 60, B. When the thin leather is dry the inlays of the leaves and flowers, &c., may be stamped out with steel punches cut to the shape of the tools; or if only a few inlays are needed, the tools may be impressed on the thin leather, and the inlays cut out with a sharp knife. The edges of the larger

Inlaying on Leather

inlays should be pared round carefully. For inlaying a panel or other large surface, the leather is pared very thin and evenly with a French knife, and a piece of paper pasted on to the grained side and left to dry. When dry, the shape of the panel, or other space to be inlaid, is marked on it through the paper pattern, and leather and paper cut through to the shape required. The edges must then be carefully pared, and the piece attached with paste, and nipped in the press to make it stick. When the paste is dry, the paper may be damped and washed off. The object of the paper is to prevent the thin leather from stretching when it is pasted.

For white inlays it is better to use Japanese paper than leather, as white leather, when pared very thin, will show the colours of the under leather through, and look dirty. If paper is used, it should be sized with vellum size before tooling.

When many dots or leaves are to be inlaid, the pieces of leather, cut out with the punch, may be laid face downwards on a paring stone, and a piece of paper, thickly covered with paste, laid on it. This, on being taken up, will carry with it the "inlays," and they can be picked up one at a time on the point of a fine folder, and stuck on the book.

Inlaying on Leather

"Inlays" of tools are attached after the pattern has been "blinded" in, and must be again worked over with the tool, in blind, when the paste is nearly dry.

On vellum an effect similar to that of inlays on leather can be obtained by the use of stains.

CHAPTER XV

Lettering—Blind Tooling—Heraldic Ornament

LETTERING ON THE BACK

Lettering on the Back

LETTERING may be done either with separate letters, each on its own handle, or with type set in a type-holder and worked across the back as a pallet. Although by the use of type great regularity is ensured, and some time saved, the use of handle letters gives so much more freedom of arrangement that their use is advocated for extra binding. Where a great many copies of the same work have to be lettered, the use of type has obvious advantages.

A great deal depends on the design of the letters used. Nearly all bookbinders' letters are made too narrow, and with too great difference between the thick and thin strokes. At fig. 90 is shown an

FIG. 90

alphabet, for which I am indebted to the kindness of Mr. Emery Walker. The long tail of the Q is meant to go under the U. It might be well to have a second R cut, with a shorter tail, to avoid the great space left when an A happens to follow it. I have found that four sizes of letters are sufficient for all books.

To make out a lettering paper for the back of a book, cut a strip of good thin paper as wide as the height of the panel to be lettered. Fold it near the centre, and mark the fold with a pencil. This should give a line exactly at right angles to the top and bottom of the strip. Then make another fold the distance from the first of the width of the back; then bring the two folds together, and make a third fold in the exact centre. The paper

Lettering on the Back

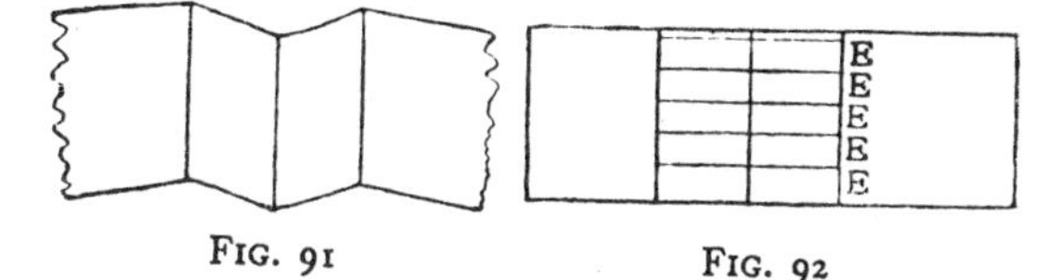

FIG. 91

FIG. 92

should then be as shown at fig. 91. Supposing the lettering to be THE WORKS OF ROBERT LOUIS STEVENSON, select the size of letter you desire to use, and take an E and mark on a piece of spare paper a line of E's, and laying your folded paper against it, see how many letters will go in comfortably. Supposing you find that four lines of five letters of the selected size can be put in, you must see if your title can be conveniently cut up into four lines of five letters, or less. It might be done as shown at fig. 93. But if you prefer not to split the

Lettering on the Back

name STEVENSON, a smaller letter must be employed, and then the lettering may be as at fig. 94.

To find out the position of the lines of lettering on a panel, the letter E is again taken and impressed five times at the side of the panel, as shown at fig. 92, leaving a little greater distance between

FIG. 93

FIG. 94

the lowest letter and the bottom of the panel, than between the letters. The paper is then folded on the centre fold, and, with dividers set to the average distance between the head of one letter and the head of the next, five points are made through the folded paper. The paper is opened, turned over, and the points joined with a fine folder worked against the straight-edge. It should leave on the front five raised lines, up to which the head of the letters must be put.

Lettering on the Back

The letters in the top line are counted, and the centre letter marked. Spaces between words are counted as a letter; thus in "THE WORKS," "W" will be the centre letter, and should be put on the paper first, and the others added on each side of it. Some thought is needed in judging where to put the centre, as the difference in the width of such letters as "M" and "W" and "I" and "J" have to be taken into account.

As a general rule, lettering looks best if it comfortably fills the panel, but of course it cannot always be made to do this. The greatest difficulty will be found in making titles of books that consist of a single word, look well. Thus if you have "CORIOLANUS" to place on a back which is not more than ⅝-inch wide, if it is put across as one word, as at fig. 95 (1), it will be illegible from the smallness of the type, and will tell merely as a gold line at a little distance. If a reasonably large type is used, the word must be broken up somewhat, as at (2), which is perhaps better, but still not at all satisfactory. The word may be put straight along the back, as at fig. (3), but this hardly looks well on a book with raised

Lettering on the Back

bands, and should be avoided unless necessary.

The use of type of different sizes in lettering a book should be avoided when possible, and on no account whatever should letters of different design be introduced. Occasionally, when the reason for

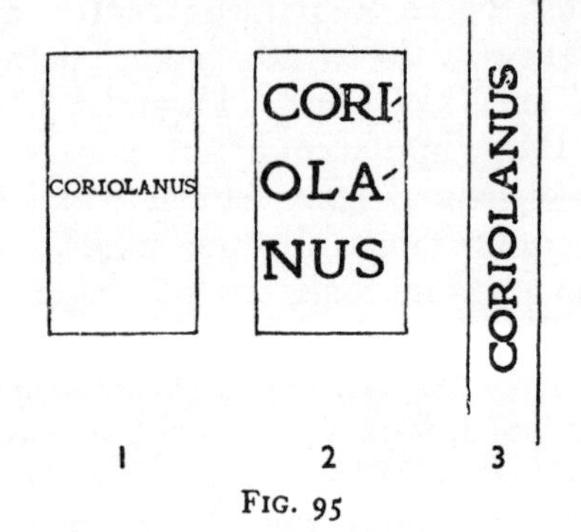

FIG. 95

it is obvious, it may be allowable to make a word shorter by putting in a small letter, supposing that only thus could reasonably large type be used. It is especially allowable in cases where, in a set of volumes, there is one much thinner than the others. It is generally better to make some compromise with the lettering of the thin volume, than to spoil the lettering of the whole set by

Lettering on the Back

using too small a letter throughout (see fig. 115).

On very thin books it is sometimes hardly possible to get any lettering at all on the back. In such cases the lettering is best put on the side.

In the case of some special books that are to have elaborately decorated bindings, and are on that account sufficiently distinct from their neighbours, a certain amount of freedom is permissible with the lettering, and a little mystery is not perhaps out of place. But in most cases books have to be recognised by their titles, and it is of the utmost importance that the lettering should be as clear as possible, and should fully identify the volume.

For lettering half-bindings and other books on which much time cannot be spared, it would take too long to make out a paper, as described for extra bindings, nor is there on such work much occasion for it. For such books the lettering should be written out carefully, the whole panel prepared and glaired in, and the gold laid on. Then with a piece of fine silk or thread lines may be marked across the gold as a guide to the finisher, and the letters worked from the centre

Lettering on the Back

outward, as described for making out the paper pattern. Of course this method does not allow of such nice calculation and adjustment as when a paper pattern is made out; but if a general principle of

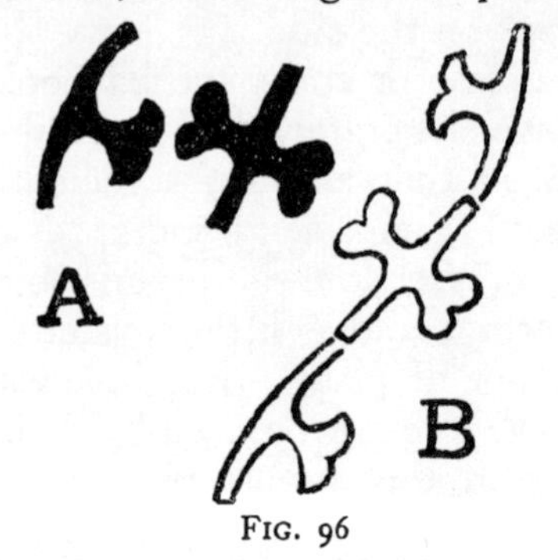

FIG. 96

clear lettering is recognised and accepted, very good results may be obtained.

BLIND TOOLING

Blind Tooling

At the end of the book characteristic examples of blind-tooled books are given (plates I–V). It will be seen that most of the tools form complete designs in themselves. Although the use of detached die-sunk tools was general, there were also simple tools used, which, when combined, made up more or less organic designs, and allowed more freedom to the finisher (see figs. 96 and 97).

Blind Tooling

Some use may also be made of interlaced strap-work designs, worked either

FIG. 97

with gouges or a small fillet. A book bound in oaken boards, with a leather back with knotted decoration, is shown in plate V. I have found that such binding and decoration are more satisfactory in schemes for old books than most forms of modern binding.

Blind Tooling

If a design is simple, the cover is marked up with dividers, and the tools impressed direct upon the leather; or, if it is elaborate, a paper pattern is made out, and the tools blinded through the paper, as described for gold tooling. The leather is then damped with water, and the impressions retooled.

The panel lines on most of the bindings before 1500 show evidence of having been put in with a tool which has been pushed along the leather, and not with a wheel. I have found that a tool guided by a straight-edge, and "jiggered" backwards and forwards, makes by far the best lines for blind-tool work. It should be borne in mind that the line is formed by the raised portion of leather, and so the tool should be cut somewhat as at fig. 98. This should leave three ridges on the leather. Blind tooling may be gone over and over until it is deep enough, and may be combined with various other methods of working. For instance, in tooling such a spray as is shown at fig. 99, the leaf would be formed by five impressions of the second tool, shown at A, the extremity of the impressions could be joined with

FIG. 98

gouges, and the stalk and veining could either be run in with a fillet or worked with gouges. The grapes would best be worked with a tool cut for the purpose. One edge of all gouge or fillet impressions can be smoothed down with some such tool as shown in section at B. This has to be worked round the gouge lines with a steady hand, and may be fairly hot if it is kept moving. At C is shown a section of a gouge impression before and after the use of this tool. The ground can be dotted in, or otherwise gone over with some small tool to throw up the pattern.

Blind Tooling

A

B C

FIG. 99

Blind tooling can sometimes be used in combination with gold tooling.

In the fifteenth century the Venetian binders used little roundels of some gesso-like substance, that were brightly coloured or gilt, in combination with blind tooling

Blind Tooling

(see plate IV). This is a method that might be revived.

What is known as "leather work" is a further development of blind tooling. This method of decoration has been revived lately, but not generally with success. "Leather work" may be divided into two branches; in one the surface of the leather is cut to outline the pattern, and in the other the leather is embossed from the back, while wet, and the pattern outlined by an indented line. Sometimes the two methods are combined. As embossing from the back necessitates the work being done before the leather is on the book, it is not very suitable for decorating books. Leather first decorated and then stuck on the book never looks as if it was an integral part of the binding. The cut leather work, which may be done after the book is bound, and leaves the surface comparatively flat, is a better method to employ for books, provided the cuts are not too deep, and are restricted to the boards, so as not to weaken the leather at the back and joints. Much of the leather used for "leather work" is of very poor quality, and will not last; for modelling it must be thick on the side of the book, and for the book to open it must be pared thin at the joint, thus making it necessary to use a thick skin very much pared down, and consequently weakened (see p. 155). Another very common fault in modelled "leather work" is that the two sides and the back are often worked separately and stuck together on the book, necessitating a join, and consequently a weak place in the hinge, where strength is most wanted. Again, in most modern "leather work," those who do the decoration do not, as a rule, do the binding, and often do not understand enough of the craft to do suitable work.

Blind Tooling

All those engaged in leather work are advised to learn to bind their own books, and to use only such methods of decoration as can be carried out on the bound book.

HERALDRY ON BOOK COVERS

It is an old and good custom to put the arms of the owner of a library on the covers of the books he has bound. The traditional way, and certainly one of the best ways, to do this is to have an arms block designed and cut. To design an arms

Heraldry on Book Covers

block, knowledge of heraldry is needed, and also some clear idea of the effect to be aimed at. A very common mistake in designing blocks is to try and get the effect of hand tooling. Blocks should be and look something entirely different. In hand tooling much of the effect is got from the impressions of small tools reflecting the light at slightly different angles, giving the work life and interest. Blocked gold, being all in one plane, has no such lights in it, and depends entirely on its design for its effect.

Provided the heraldry identifies the owner, it should be as simply drawn as it can be; the custom of indicating the tinctures by lines and dots on the charges generally makes a design confused, obscuring the coat it is intended to make clear. In designing heraldic blocks, it is well to get a good deal of solid flat surface of gold to make the blocked design stand out from any gold-tooled work on the cover.

Another way of putting armorial bearings on covers is to paint them in oil paint. In the early sixteenth century the Venetians copied the Eastern custom of sinking panels in their book covers, and painted coats of arms on these sunk portions very successfully. The ground-work of the shield itself was usually raised a little, either by something under the leather, or by some gesso-like substance on its surface.

Heraldry on Book Covers

Arms blocks should be placed a little above the centre of the cover. Generally, if the centre of the block is in a line with the centre band of a book with five bands, it will look right.

Blocks are struck with the aid of an arming or blocking press. The block is attached to the movable plate of the press called the "platen." To do this some stout brown paper is first glued to the platen, and the block glued to this, and the platen fixed in its place at the bottom of the heating-box. In blocking arms on a number of books of different sizes, some nice adjustment of the movable bed is needed to get the blocks to fall in exactly the right place.

For blocking, one coat of glaire will be enough for most leathers. The gold is laid on as for hand tooling. The block should be brought down and up again fairly sharply. The heat needed is about the same as for hand tooling.

CHAPTER XVI

Designing for Gold-tooled Decoration

DESIGNING TOOLS

Designing for Gold-tooled Decoration

FOR gold tooling, such tools as gouges, dots, pieces of straight line, and fillets are to be had ready-made at most dealers. Other tools are best designed and cut to

FIG. 100 (reduced)

order. At first only a few simple forms will be needed, such as one or two flowers of different sizes, and one or two sets of leaves (see fig. 100).

In designing tools, it must be borne in mind that they may appear on the book many times repeated, and so must be simple in outline and much conventionalised. A more or less naturalistic drawing of a flower, showing the natural irregularities, may look charming, but if a tool is cut from it, any marked irregularity becomes extremely annoying when repeated several times on a cover. So with leaves, unless they are perfectly symmetrical, there should be three of each shape cut, two curving in different directions, and the third quite straight (see fig. 101). To have only one leaf, and to have that curved, produces very restless patterns. The essence of gold-tool design is that patterns are made up of repeats of impressions of tools,

Designing for Gold-tooled Decoration

FIG. 101

and that being so, the tools must be so designed that they will repeat pleasantly, and in practice it will be found that any but simple forms will become aggressive in repetition.

Designs for tools should be made out with Indian ink on white paper, and they may be larger than the size of the required tool. The tool-cutter will reduce any drawing to any desired size, and will, from one drawing, cut any number of tools of different sizes. Thus, if a set of

Designing for Gold-tooled Decoration

five leaves of the same shape is wanted, it will only be necessary to draw one, and to indicate the sizes the others are to be in some such way as shown at fig. 102.

It is not suggested that special tools should be cut for each pattern, but the need of new tools will naturally arise from time to time, and so the stock be gradually increased. It is better to begin with a very few, and add a tool or two as

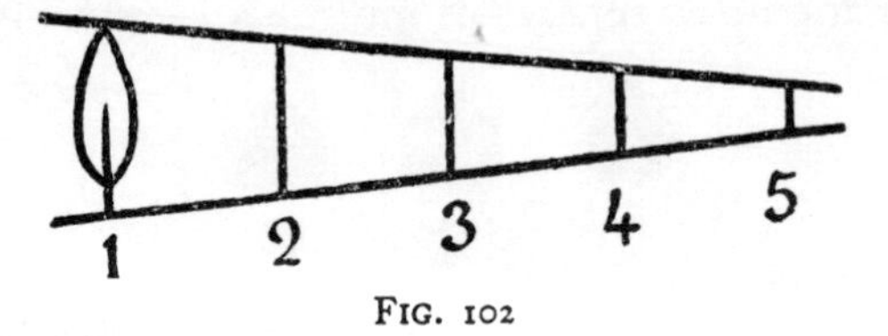

FIG. 102

occasion arises, than to try to design a complete set when starting.

Tools may be solid or in outline. If in outline they may be used as "inlay" tools, and in ordering them the tool-cutter should be asked to provide steel punches for cutting the inlays.

Combining Tools to Form Patterns

COMBINING TOOLS TO FORM PATTERNS

It is well for the student to begin with patterns arranged on some very simple plan, making slight changes in each succeeding pattern. In this way an individual style may be established. The usual plan of studying the perfected styles of the old binders, and trying to begin where they left off, in practice only leads to the production of exact imitations, or poor lifeless parodies, of the old designs. Whereas a pattern developed by the student by slow degrees, through a series of designs, each slightly different from the one before it, will, if eccentricities are avoided, probably have life and individual interest.

Combining Tools to Form Patterns

Perhaps the easiest way to decorate a binding is to cover it with some small repeating pattern. A simple form of diaper as a beginning is shown at fig. 104. To make such a pattern, cut a piece of good, thin paper to the size of the board of a book, and with a pencil rule a line about an eighth of an inch inside the margin all round. Then with the point of a fine folder that will indent, but not cut the paper, mark up as shown in fig. 103. The position of the lines A A and B B is found by simply folding the paper, first side to side, and then head to tail. The other lines can be put in without any

Combining Tools to Form Patterns

measurement by simply joining all points where lines cross. By continual re-crossing, the spaces into which the paper is divided can be reduced to any desired size. If the construction lines are accurately put in, the spaces will all be of the same size and shape. It is then evident that a

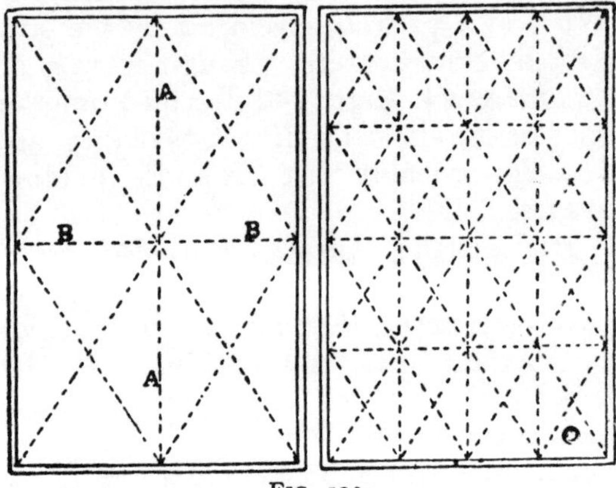

FIG. 103

repeating design to fill any one of the spaces can be made to cover the whole surface.

In fig. 104, it is the diagonal lines only that are utilised for the pattern. To avoid confusion, the cross lines that helped to determine the position of the diagonals are not shown.

Combining Tools to Form Patterns

FIG. 104 (reduced)

Combining Tools to Form Patterns

The advantage of using the point of a folder to mark up the constructional lines of a pattern instead of a pencil, is that the lines so made are much finer, do not rub out, and do not cause confusion by interfering with the pattern. Any lines that will appear on the book, such as the marginal lines, may be put in with a pencil to distinguish them.

Having marked up the paper, select a flower tool and impress it at the points where the diagonal lines cross, holding it in the smoke of a candle between every two or three impressions. When the flower has been impressed all over, select a small piece of straight line, and put a stalk in below each flower; then a leaf put in on each side of the straight line will complete the pattern.

A development of the same principle is shown at fig. 105, in which some gouges are introduced. Any number of other combinations will occur to any one using the tools. Frequently questions will arise as to whether a tool is to be put this way or that way, and whether a line is to curve up or down. Whenever there is such an alternative open, there is the germ of another pattern. All-over diaper patterns

FIG. 105 (reduced)

Combining Tools to Form Patterns

may be varied in any number of ways. One way is to vary the design in alternate spaces. If this is done one of the designs should be such that it will divide down the centre both ways and so finish off the pattern comfortably at the edges. The pattern may be based on the upright and the cross-lines of the marking up, or the marking up may be on a different principle altogether. The designer, after a little practice, will be bewildered by the infinite number of combinations that occur to him.

The diaper is selected for a beginning because it is the easiest form of pattern to make, as there is no question of getting round corners, and very little of studying proportion. It is selected also because it teaches the student the decorative value of simple forms repeated on some orderly system. When he has grasped this, he has grasped the underlying principle of nearly all successful tooled ornament. Diapers are good practice, because in a close, all-over pattern the tools must be put down in definite places, or an appalling muddle will result. In tooling, a repeat of the same few tools is the best possible practice, giving as it does the same work

FIG. 106 (reduced)

Combining Tools to Form Patterns

over and over again under precisely the same conditions, and concentrating, on one book cover, the practice that might be spread over several backs and sides more sparingly decorated, when variety of conditions would confuse the student.

FIG. 107

When the principles of the diaper have been mastered, and the student has become familiar with the limitations of his tools, other schemes of decoration may be attempted, such as borders, centres, or panels.

A form of border connected with cross-lines is shown at fig. 106. This is made up of a repeat of the spray built up of three tools and four gouges shown at fig. 107, with slight modification at the corners. Other schemes for borders are those in which flowers grow inwards from the edge of the boards, or outwards from a panel at the centre, or on both sides of a line about half an inch from the edge. A pattern may also be made to grow all round the centre panel. Borders will be found more difficult to manage than simple diapers, and at first, are best built up on the same principle—the repeat of some simple element.

Combining Tools to Form Patterns

The decoration may be concentrated on parts of the cover, such as the centre or corners. A design for a centre is shown at fig. 108, and below is shown the way to construct it. A piece of paper is folded, as shown by the dotted lines, and an eighth of the pattern drawn with a soft pencil and folded over on the line A, and transferred by being rubbed at the back with a folder. This is lined in with a pencil, and folded over on the line B and rubbed off. This is lined in and folded over on A and C, rubbed off as before, and the whole lined in. The overs and unders of the lines are then marked, and gouges selected to fit. Of course it will take several trials before the lines will interlace pleasantly, and the tools fit in. Another centre, in which a spray is repeated three times, is shown at fig. 109, and any number of others will occur to the student after a little practice. A change of tools, or the slight alteration of a line, will give an entirely new aspect to a pattern. In plate VII is shown an all-over pattern growing from the bottom centre of the board. In this design the leather was

Combining Tools to Form Patterns

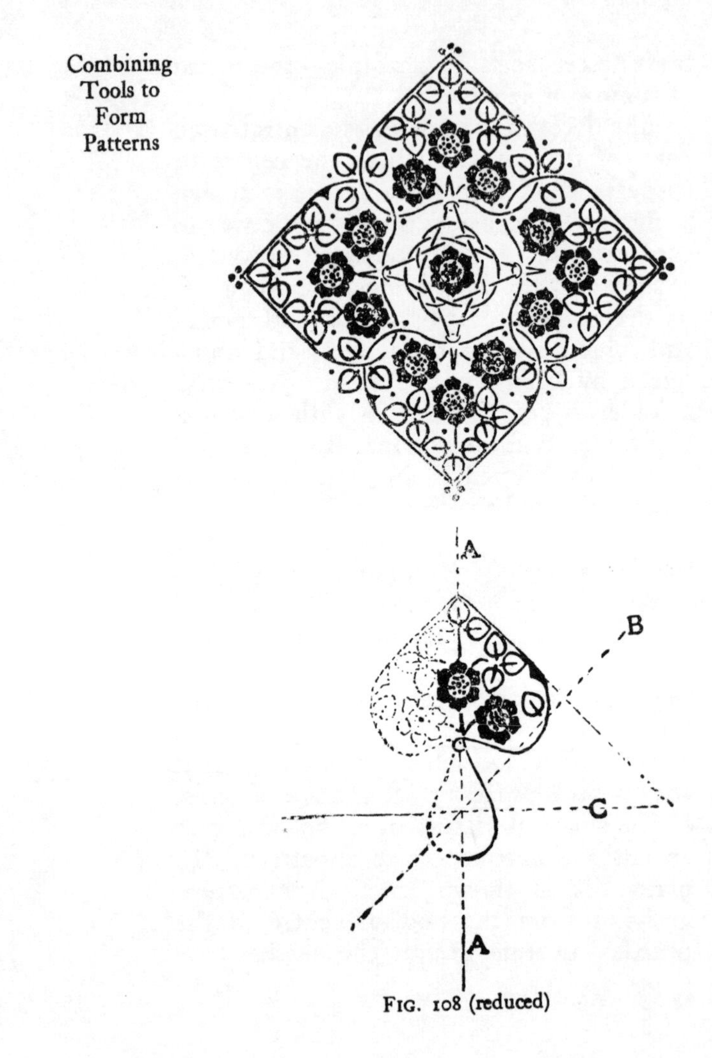

FIG. 108 (reduced)

dark green, with a lighter green panel in the centre. The berries were inlaid in bright red. Although at first glance it seems an intricate design, it is made up like the others of repetitions of simple forms.

Combining Tools to Form Patterns

When the student has become proficient in the arrangement of tools in

FIG. 109 (reduced)

combination with lines, a design consisting entirely, or almost entirely, of lines may be tried. This is more difficult, because the limitations are not so obvious; but here again the principle of repetition and even distribution should be followed. At fig. 110 is shown a design almost entirely composed of lines, built up on the same principle as the centre at fig. 108.

The ends of the bands form a very

Combining Tools to Form Patterns

pleasant starting-place for patterns. In plates V–VII are shown ways of utilising this method. To look right, a pattern

FIG. 110 (reduced)

Combining Tools to Form Patterns

must be consistent throughout. The tools and their arrangement must have about the same amount of convention. Gold tooling, dealing, as it does, with flat forms in silhouette only, necessitates very considerable formality in the design of the tools and of their arrangement on the cover. Modern finishers have become so skilful that they are able to produce in gold tooling almost any design that can be drawn in lines with a pencil, and some truly marvellous results are obtained by the use of inlays, and specially cut gouges. As a rule, such patterns simply serve to show the skill of the finisher, and to make one wonder who could have been foolish enough to select so limited and laborious a method as gold tooling for carrying them out.

Generally speaking, successful gold-tooled patterns show evidence of having been designed with the tools; of being, in fact, mere arrangements of the tools, and not of having been first designed with a pencil, and then worked with tools cut to fit the drawing. This does not of course apply to patterns composed entirely of lines, or to patterns composed of lines of dots.

Combining Tools to Form Patterns

If artists wish to design for gold tooling without first mastering the details, probably the safest way will be for them to design in lines of gold dots. Some successful patterns carried out in this way were shown at the Arts and Crafts Exhibition some years ago.

Designs for gold-tooled binding should always be constructed on some geometrical plan, and whatever pattern there is symmetrically distributed over the cover.

If lettering can be introduced, it will be found to be most useful when arranging a pattern. It gives dignity and purpose to a design, and is also highly decorative. Lettering may be arranged in panels, as in plate VI, or in a border round the edge of the board, and in many other ways. It may either consist of the title of the book, or some line or verse from it or connected with it, or may refer to its history, or to the owner. Anything that gives a personal interest to a book, such as the arms of the owner, the initials or name of the giver or receiver of a present, with perhaps the date of the gift, is of value.

The use of the small fillet makes it possible to employ long, slightly-curved

Combining Tools to Form Patterns

lines. Gold-tooled lines have in themselves such great beauty that designers are often tempted to make them meander about the cover in a weak and aimless way. As the limitations enforced by the use of gouges tend to keep the curves strong and small, and as the use of the

FIG. 111

small fillet tends to the production of long, weak curves, students are advised at first to restrict the curved lines in their patterns to such as can be readily worked with gouges.

It must be remembered that a gouge or fillet line is very thin, and will look weak if it goes far without support. For this reason interlaced lines are advocated.

Gouge lines are easier to work, and look better if a small space is left where the gouges end. This is especially the

Combining Tools to Form Patterns

case where lines bearing leaves or flowers branch from the main stem (see fig. 111).

Gouges and fillets need not always be of the same thickness of line, and two or three sets of different gauges may be kept. A finisher can always alter the thickness of a gouge with emery paper.

One method of arranging gold-tooled

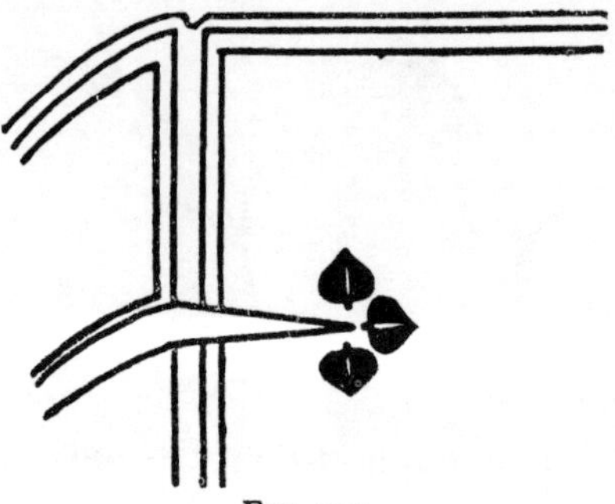

FIG. 112

lines is to treat them in design as if they were wires in tension, and knot and twist them together. Provided the idea is consistently adhered to throughout, such a pattern is often very successful.

A simple arrangement of straight lines will be sufficient ornamentation for most books. Three schemes for such ornamentation are shown. In fig. 112 the "tie downs" may be in "blind" and the lines in gold. The arrangement

Combining Tools to Form Patterns

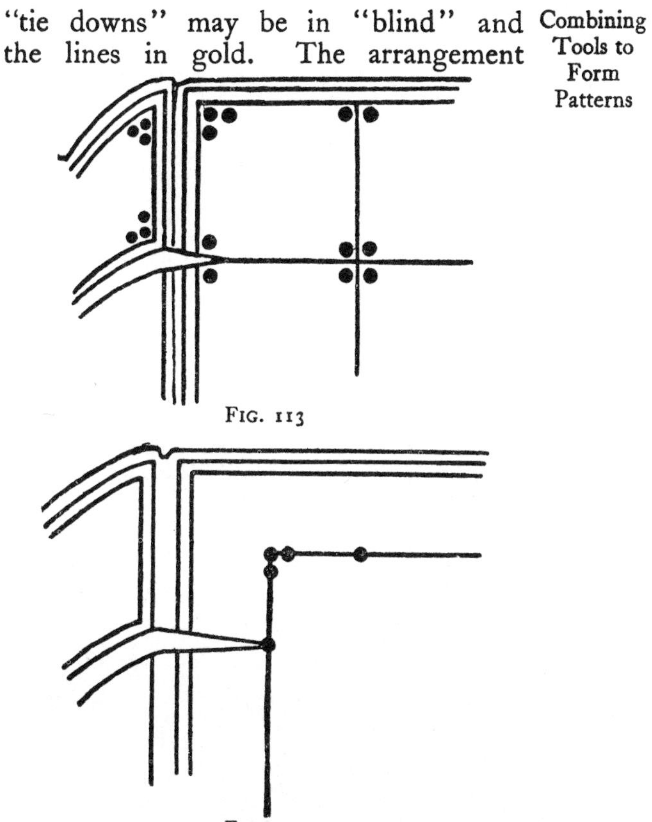

Fig. 113

Fig. 114

shown at fig. 113 leaves a panel at the top which may be utilised for lettering.

Combining Tools to Form Patterns

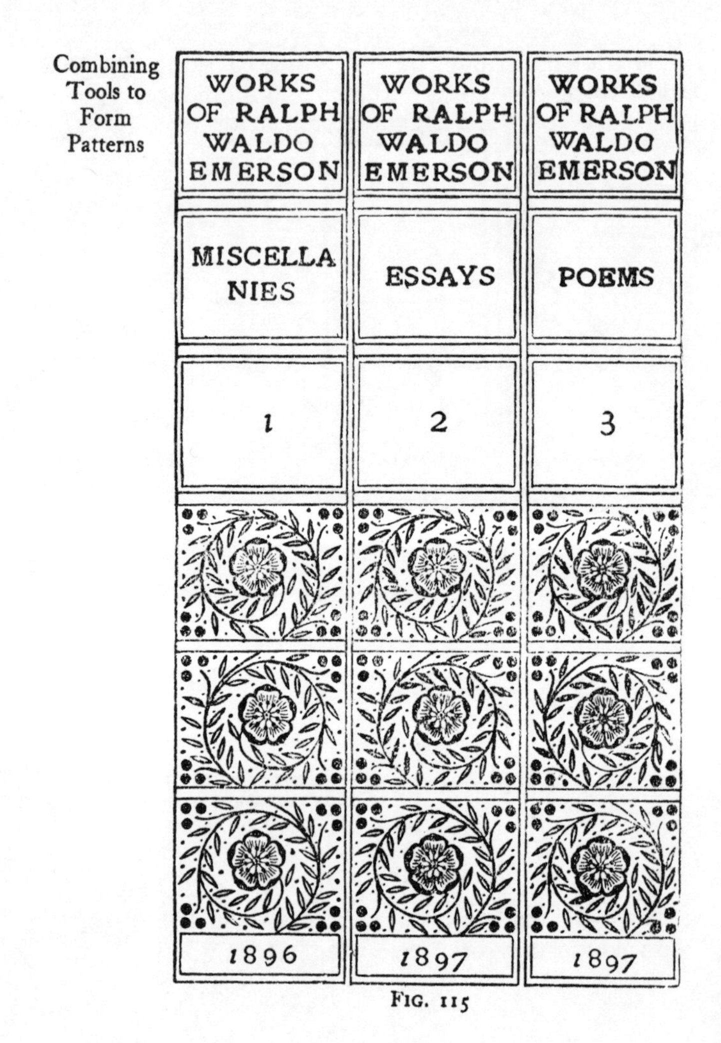

FIG. 115

Combining Tools to Form Patterns

FIG. 115

Combining Tools to Form Patterns

DESIGNING FOR BACKS

The decoration of the back of a book is difficult owing to the very small space usually available in the panels. The first consideration must be the lettering, and when that has been arranged, as described in Chapter XV, a second paper is got out for the pattern. The back panel should generally be treated in the same style and, if possible, with the same tools as the sides, if they are decorated. It will often be found far easier to design a full-gilt side than a satisfactory back.

A design may be made to fit one panel of the book and repeated on all those not required for lettering (see plates VI and VII), or it may be made to grow up from panel to panel (see fig. 115). In the case of sets of books in which the volumes vary very much in thickness, some pattern must be made that can be contracted and expanded without altering the general look of the back (see fig. 115).

DESIGNING FOR INSIDE OF BOARDS

The inside margins of the board permit of a little delicate decoration. At fig. 116 are shown two ways of treating this part of the binding. The inside of the board is sometimes covered all over with leather,

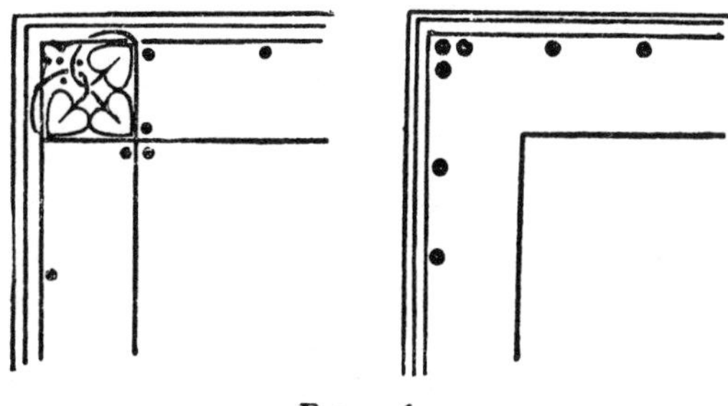

FIG. 116

and tooled as elaborately as, or more elaborately than, the outside. If there are vellum ends, they may be enriched with a little tooling.

The edges of the boards may have a gold line run on them, and the head-cap may be decorated with a few dots.

CHAPTER XVII

Pasting Down End Papers—Opening Books

PASTING DOWN END PAPERS

Pasting Down End Papers

WHEN the finishing is done, the end papers should be pasted down on to the board; or if there is a leather joint, the panel left should be filled in to match the end paper.

To paste down end papers, the book is placed on the block with the board open (see fig. 117, A), the waste sheets are torn off, the joints cleared of any glue or paste, and the boards flattened, as described at page 171 for pasting down leather joints. One of the paste-down papers is then stretched over the board and rubbed down in the joint, and the amount to be cut off to make it fit into the space left by the turn-in of the leather is marked on it with dividers, measuring from the edge of the board. A cutting tin is then placed on the book, the paste-down paper turned over it, and the edges trimmed off to the divider points with a knife and straight-edge, leaving small pieces to cover the ends of the joint (fig. 117, A c).

Pasting Down End Papers

The cutting and pasting down of these small pieces in the joint are rather difficult;

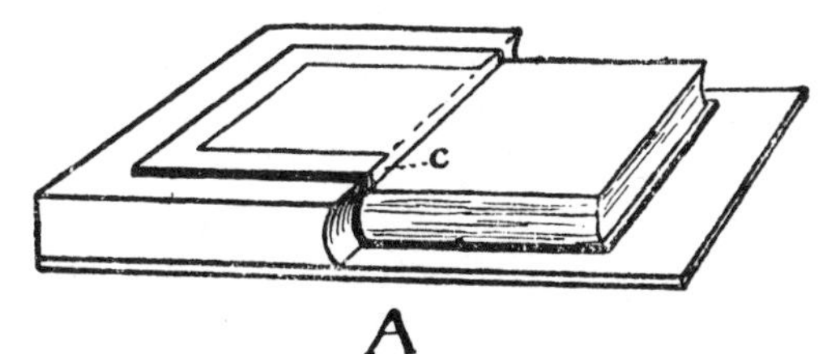

A

B

FIG. 117

they should come exactly to the edges of the board.

When both paste-down papers are trimmed to size, one of them is well pasted with thin paste in which there

Pasting Down End Papers

are no lumps, with a piece of waste paper under it to protect the book. The joints should also be pasted, and the paste rubbed in with the finger and any surplus removed.

The pasted paper is then brought over on to the board, the edges adjusted exactly to their places, and rubbed down. The joint must next be rubbed down through paper. It is difficult to get the paper to stick evenly in the joint, and great nicety is needed here. All rubbing down must be done through paper, or the "paste-down" will be soiled or made shiny.

Some papers stretch very much when pasted, and will need to be cut a little smaller than needed, and put down promptly after pasting. Thin vellum may be put down with paste in which there is a very little glue, but thicker vellum is better put down with thin glue. In pasting vellum, very great care is needed to prevent the brush-marks from showing through. If the vellum is thin, the board must be lined with white or toned paper with a smooth surface. This paper must be quite clean, as any marks will show through the vellum, and make it look dirty.

When one side is pasted down the book

can be turned over without shutting the board, and the other board opened and pasted down in the same way (see fig. 117, B). In turning over a book, a piece of white paper should be put under the newly pasted side, as, being damp, it will soil very readily. When both ends have been pasted down the joints should be examined and rubbed down again, and the book stood up on end with the boards open until the end papers are dry. The boards may be held open with a piece of cardboard cut as shown at fig. 71.

Pasting Down End Papers

If there are cloth joints they are put down with glue, and the board paper is placed nearly to the edge of the joint, leaving very little cloth visible.

In the process of finishing, the boards of a book will nearly always be warped a little outward, but the pasted end papers should draw the boards a little as they dry, causing them to curve slightly towards the book. With vellum ends there is a danger that the boards will be warped too much.

OPENING NEWLY BOUND BOOKS

Opening Newly Bound Books

Before sending out a newly bound book the binder should go through it, opening

Opening Newly Bound Books

it here and there to ease the back. The volume is laid on a table, and the leaves opened a short distance from the front, and then at an equal distance from the back, and then in one or two places nearer the centre of the book, the leaves being pressed down with the hand at each opening. If the book is a valuable one, every leaf should then be turned over separately and each opening pressed down, beginning from the centre and working first one way and then the other. In this way the back will be bent evenly at all points. When a book has been opened, it should be lightly pressed for a short time without anything in the joints.

If a book is sent out unopened, the first person into whose hands it falls will probably open it somewhere in the centre, bending the covers back and "breaking" the back; and if any leaves chance to have been stuck together in edge-gilding, they are likely to be torn if carelessly opened. A book with a "broken" back will always have a tendency to open in the same place, and will not keep its shape. It would be worth while for librarians to have newly bound books carefully opened. An assistant could "open" a large number of books in a day, and the benefit to the bindings would amply compensate for the small trouble and cost involved.

Opening Newly Bound Books

CHAPTER XVIII

Clasps and Ties—Metal on Bindings

CLASPS AND TIES

Clasps and Ties

SOME books need to be clasped to keep the leaves flat. All books written or printed on vellum should have clasps. Vellum unless kept flat is apt to cockle, and this in a book will force the leaves apart and admit dust. If a book is tightly wedged in a shelf the leaves will be kept flat, but as the chance removal of any other book from the row will remove the pressure, it is much better to provide clasps for vellum books.

Very thick books, and those with a great many folded plates, are better for having clasps to prevent the leaves from sagging. As nearly all books are now kept in bookshelves, and as any projection on the side of a book is likely to injure the neighbouring volume, a form of clasp should be used that has no raised parts on the boards.

At fig. 118 is shown a simple clasp suitable for small books with mill-board sides, with details of the metal parts, made of thick silver wire, below. Double boards must be "made," and the flattened ends of the silver catch inserted between the two thicknesses, and glued in place. About one-eighth of an inch of the end should project. In covering, the leather must be pierced and carefully worked round the catch. To make the plait, three strips of thin leather are slipped through the ring, and the ends of each strip pasted together. The three doubled strips are then plaited and the end of the plait put through a hole in the lower board of the book about half an inch from the edge, and glued down inside. A groove may be cut in the mill-board from the hole to the edge before covering, to make a

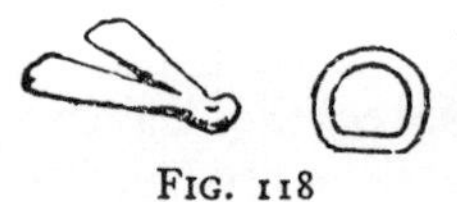

Fig. 118

depression in which the plait will lie, and a depression may be scooped out of the inner surface of the board to receive the ends.

At fig. 119 is a somewhat similar clasp with three plaits suitable for large books. The metal end and the method of inserting it into wooden boards are shown below. The turned-down end should go right through the board, and be riveted on the inside. When the three plaits are worked, a little band of silver may be riveted on just below the ring.

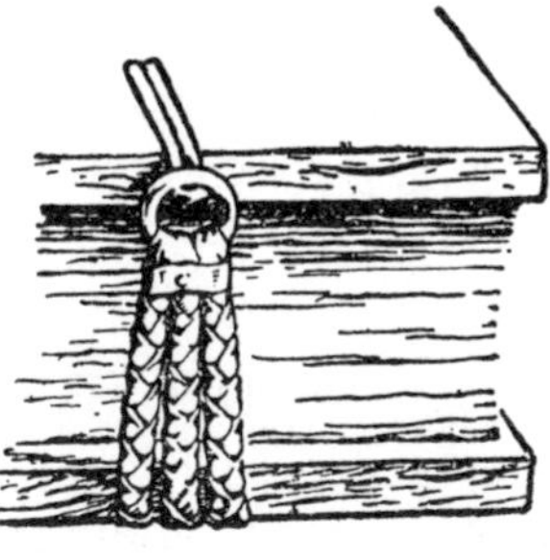

FIG. 119

A very simple fastening that is sometimes useful is shown at fig. 77. A very small bead is threaded on to a piece of catgut, and the two ends of the gut brought together and put through a larger bead. The ends of the gut with the beads on them are laced into the top

Clasps and Ties

board of the book, with the bead projecting over the edge, and a loop of gut is laced into the bottom board. If the loop can be made exactly the right length, this is a serviceable method.

Silk or leather ties may be used to keep books shut, but they are apt to be in the way when the book is read, and as hardly anybody troubles to tie them, they are generally of very little use.

METAL ON BINDINGS

Metal on Bindings

Metal corners and bosses are a great protection to bindings, but if the books are to go into shelves, the metal must be quite smooth and flat. A metal shoe on the lower edge of the boards is an excellent thing for preserving the binding of heavy books.

Bosses and other raised metal work should be restricted to books that will be used on lecterns or reading desks. The frontispiece is from a drawing of an early sixteenth-century book, bound in white pigskin, and ornamented with brass corners, centres, and clasps; and in plate I is shown a fifteenth-century binding with plain protecting bosses. On this book there were originally five bosses on each board, but the centre ones have been lost.

Metal on Bindings

Bindings may be entirely covered with metal, but the connection between the binding and the book is in that case seldom quite satisfactory. The most satisfactory metal-covered bindings that I have seen are those in which the metal is restricted to the boards. The book is bound in wooden boards, with thick leather at the back, and plaques of metal nailed to the wood. The metal may be set with jewels or decorated with enamel, and embossed or chased in various ways.

Jewels are sometimes set in invisible settings below the leather of bindings, giving them the appearance of being set in the leather. This gives them an insecure look, and it is better frankly to show the metal settings and make a decorative feature of them.

CHAPTER XIX

Leather

LEATHER

Leather

Of all the materials used by the bookbinder, leather is the most important

Leather

and the most difficult to select wisely. It is extremely difficult to judge a leather by its appearance.

"We find now, that instead of leather made from sheep, calf, goat, and pigskins, each having, when finished, its own characteristic surface, sheepskins are got up to look like calf, morocco, or pigskin; calf is grained to resemble morocco, or so polished and flattened as to have but little character left; while goatskins are grained in any number of ways, and pigskin is often grained like levant morocco. So clever are some of these imitations that it takes a skilled expert to identify a leather when it is on a book."

There have been complaints for a long time of the want of durability of modern bookbinding leather, but there has not been until lately any systematic investigation into the causes of its premature decay.

By permission, I shall quote largely from the report of the committee appointed by the Society of Arts to inquire into the subject. There are on this special committee leather manufacturers, bookbinders, librarians, and owners of libraries. The report issued is the result of an immense amount of work done. Many libraries were visited, and hundreds of experiments and tests were carried out by the sub-committees. There is much useful information in the report that all bookbinders and librarians should read. The work of the committee is not yet finished, but its findings may be accepted as conclusive as far as they go.

The committee first set themselves to ascertain if the complaints of the premature decay of modern bookbinding leather are justified by facts, and on this point report that—

"As regards the common belief that modern binding leather does decay prematurely, the sub-committee satisfied themselves that books bound during the last eighty or hundred years showed far greater evidence of deterioration than those of an earlier date. Many recent bindings showed evidence of decay after so short a period as ten or even five years. The sub-committee came to the conclusion that there is ample justification for the general complaint that modern leather is not so durable as that formerly used. To fix the date of the commencement of this deterioration was a difficult matter; but they came to the conclusion that while leather of all periods showed some signs of decay, the deterioration becomes more general on books bound after 1830, while some leathers seem to be generally good until about 1860, after which date nearly all leathers seem to get worse. The deterioration of calf bindings at the latter end of the 19th century may be attributed as much to the excessive thinness as to the poor quality of the material."

The committee endeavoured to ascertain the relative durability of the leathers used for bookbinding, and after visiting many libraries, and comparing bindings, they report as follows—

"As to the suitability of various leathers, the sub-committee came to the conclusion that of the old leathers (15th and 16th century), white pigskin, probably alum "tanned," is the most durable, but its excessive hardness and want of flexibility renders this leather unsuitable for most modern work. Old brown calf has lasted fairly well, but loses its flexibility, and becomes stiff and brittle when exposed to light and air. Some of the white tawed skins of the 15th and 16th century, other than white pigskin, and probably deerskin, have lasted very well. Some 15th and 16th century sheepskin bindings have remained soft and flexible, but the surface is soft, and usually much damaged by friction. Vellum seems to have lasted fairly well, but is easily influenced by atmospheric changes, and is much affected by light. Early specimens of red morocco from the 16th to the end of the 18th century were found in good condition, and of all the leathers noticed, this seems to be the least affected by the various conditions to which it had been subjected. In the opinion of the committee, most of this leather has been tanned with sumach or some closely allied tanning material. Morocco bindings earlier than 1860 were generally found to be in fairly good condition, but morocco after that date seems to be much less reliable, and in many cases has become utterly rotten. During the latter part of the 18th century it became customary to pare down calf until it was as thin as paper. Since about 1830 hardly any really sound calf seems to have been used, as, whether thick or thin, it appears generally to have perished. Sheepskin

Leather

bindings of the early part of the century are many of them still in good condition. Since about 1860 sheepskin as sheepskin is hardly to be found. Sheepskins are grained in imitation of other leathers, and these imitation-grained leathers are generally found to be in a worse condition than any of the other bindings, except, perhaps, some of the very thin calfskin. Undyed modern pigskin seems to last well, but some coloured pigskin bindings had entirely perished. Modern leathers dyed with the aid of sulphuric acid are all to be condemned. In nearly every case Russia leather was found to have become rotten, at least in bindings of the last fifty years."

On the question of the causes of the decay noticed and the best methods of preparing leather in the future, I may quote the following—

"The work of a sub-committee, which was composed of chemists specially conversant with the treatment of leather, was directed specially to the elucidation of the following points: an investigation of the nature of the decay of leather used for bookbinding; an examination of the causes which produced this decay; a research into the best methods of preparing leather for bookbinding; and a consideration of the points required to be dealt with in the preservation of books.

Leather

"Taking these points in order, the first one dealt with is the question of the nature of the decay of leather. To arrive at their conclusions on this subject, the sub-committee made a number of tests and analyses of samples of decayed leather bookbindings, as well as of leathers used for binding. The committee found that the most prevalent decay was what they term a red decay, and this they think may be differentiated into old and new, the old red decay being noticeable up to about 1830, and the new decay since that date. In the old decay, the leather becomes hard and brittle, the surface not being easily abraded by friction. The older form is specially noticeable in calf-bound books, tanned presumably with oak bark. The new form affects nearly all leathers, and in extreme cases seems absolutely to destroy the fibres. Another form of deterioration, more noticeable in the newer books, renders the grain of the leather liable to peel off when exposed to the slightest friction. This is the most common form of decay noted in the more recent leathers. In nearly all samples of Russia leather a very violent form of red decay was noticed. In many cases the leather was found to be absolutely rotten in all parts exposed to light and air, so that on the very slightest rubbing with a blunt instrument the leather fell into fine dust. . . .

"The second point is the cause of the decay. An extensive series of experiments was carried out with a view of determining the causes of the decay of bindings. The sub-committee find that this is caused by both mechanical and chemical influences. Of the latter, some are due to mistakes of the leather manufacturer and the bookbinder, others to the want of ventilation, and to improper heating and lighting of libraries. In some cases inferior leathers are finished (by methods in themselves injurious) so as to imitate the better class leathers, and of course where these are used durability cannot be expected. But in the main the injury for which the manufacturer and bookbinder are responsible must be attributed rather to ignorance of the effect of the means employed to give the leather the outward qualities required for binding than to the intentional production of an inferior article. . . . Leathers produced by different tanning materials, although they may be equally sound and durable mechanically, vary very much in their resistance to other influences, such as light, heat, and gas fumes.

"For bookbinding purposes, the sub-committee generally condemn the use of tanning materials belonging to the catechol group, although the leathers produced by the use of these materials are for many purposes excellent, and indeed superior. The class of tanning materials which produce the most suitable leather for this particular purpose belong to the pyrogallol group, of which a well-known and important example is sumach. East Indian or 'Persian' tanned sheep and goat skins, which are suitable for many purposes, and are now used largely for cheap bookbinding purposes, are considered extremely bad. Books bound in these materials have been found to show signs of decay in less than twelve months, and the sub-committee are inclined to believe that no book bound in these leathers, exposed on a shelf to sunlight or gas fumes, can ever be expected to last more than five or six years. Embossing leather under heavy pressure to imitate a grain has a very injurious effect, while the shaving of thick skins greatly reduces the strength of the leather by cutting away the tough fibres of the inner part of the skin. The use of mineral acids in brightening the colour of leather, and in the process of dyeing, has a serious effect in lessening its resistance to decay. A good deal yet remains to be learned about the relative permanency of the different dyes."

On analysis free sulphuric acid was found to be present in nearly all bookbinding leather, and it is the opinion of the committee that even a small quantity of this acid materially lessens the durability of the leather.

"It has been shown by careful experiment that even a minute quantity of sulphuric acid used in the dye bath to liberate the colour is at once absorbed by the leather, and that no amount of subsequent washing will remove it. In a very large proportion of cases the decay of modern sumach-tanned leather has been due to the sulphuric acid used in the dye bath, and retained in the skin. We have examined very many samples of leather manufactured and sold specially for bookbinding purposes, from different factories, bought from different dealers, or kindly supplied by bookbinders and by librarians, and have found them to contain, in a large number of cases, free sulphuric acid, from 0·5 up to 1·6 per cent."

The publication of the report should tend to fix a standard for bookbinding leather. Hitherto there has been no recognised standard. Bookbinders have selected leather almost entirely by its appearance. It has now been shown that appearance is no test of durability, and the mechanical test of tearing the leather is insufficient. Sound leather should tear with difficulty, and the torn edges should be fringed with long, silky fibres, and any leather which tears very easily, and shows short, curled-up fibres at the torn edges, should be discarded. But though good bookbinding leather will tear with difficulty, and show long fibres where torn, that is in itself not a sufficient test; because it has been shown that the leather that is mechanically the strongest is not necessarily the most durable and the best able to resist the adverse influences to which books are subject in libraries.

The report shows that bookbinders and librarians are not, as a general rule, qualified to select leather for bookbinding. In the old days, when the manufacture of leather was comparatively simple, a bookbinder might reasonably be expected to know enough of the processes employed to be able to select his leather. But now so complicated is the manufacture, and so many are the factors to be considered, that an expert should be employed.

"The committee have satisfied themselves that it is possible to test any leather in such a way as to guarantee its suitability for bookbinding. They have not come to any decision as to the desirability of establishing any formal or official standard, though they consider that this is a point which well deserves future consideration."

It is to be hoped that some system of examining and hall-marking leather by some recognised body may be instituted. If librarians will specify that the leather to be employed must be certified to be manufactured according to the recommendations of the Society of Arts

Committee, there is no reason why leathers should not be obtained as durable as any ever produced. This would necessitate the examining and testing of batches of leather by experts. At present this can be done more or less privately at various places, such as the Yorkshire College, Leeds, or the Herold's Institute, Bermondsey. In the near future it is to be hoped that some recognised public body, such as one of the great City Companies interested in leather, may be induced to establish a standard, and to test such leathers as are submitted to them, hall-marking those that come up to the standard. This would enable bookbinders and librarians, in ordering leather, to be sure that it had not been injured in its manufacture. The testing, if done by batches, should not add greatly to the cost of the leather.

On the question of the qualities of an ideal bookbinding leather the committee report—

"It is the opinion of the committee that the ideal bookbinding leather must have, and retain, great flexibility. . . . (It) must have a firm grain surface, not easily damaged by friction and should not be artificially grained. . . . The committee is of opinion that a pure sumach tannage will answer all these conditions, and that leather can, and will, be now produced that will prove to be as durable as any made in the past."

The committee has so far only dealt with vegetable-tanned leather. I have used, with some success, chrome-tanned calfskin. Chrome leather is difficult to pare, and to work, as it does not become soft when wet, like vegetable-tanned leather. It will stand any reasonable degree of heat, and so might perhaps be useful for top-shelf bindings and for shelf edging. It is extremely strong mechanically, but without further tests I cannot positively recommend it except for trial.

While the strength and probable durability of leather can only be judged by a trained leather chemist, there remains for the binder's selection the kind of leather to use, and its colour.

Most of the leather prepared for bookbinding is too highly finished. The finishing processes add a good deal to the cost of the leather, and are apt to be injurious to it, and as much of the high finish is lost in covering, it would be better for the bookbinder to get rougher leather and finish it himself when it is on the book.

The leathers in common use for bookbinding are—

Goatskin, known as morocco.

Calf, known as calf and russia.

Sheepskin, known as roan, basil, skiver, &c.

Pigskin, known as pigskin.

Sealskin, known as seal.

Morocco is probably the best leather for extra binding if properly prepared, but experiment has shown that the expensive Levant moroccos are nearly always ruined in their manufacture. A great many samples of the most expensive Levant morocco were tested, with the result that they were all found to contain free sulphuric acid.

Calf.—Modern vegetable-tanned calf has now become a highly unsatisfactory material, and until some radical changes are made in the methods of manufacturing it, it should not be used for bookbinding.

Sheepskin.—A properly tanned sheepskin makes a very durable, though rather soft and woolly, leather. Much of the bookbinding leather now made from sheepskin is quite worthless. Bookbinders should refuse to have anything to do with any leather that has been artificially grained, as the process is apt to be highly injurious to the skin.

Pigskin.—Pigskin is a thoroughly good leather naturally, and very strong, especially the alumed skins; but many of the dyed pigskins are found to be improperly tanned and dyed, and worthless for bookbinding.

Sealskin is highly recommended by at least one eminent librarian, and I have lately used it extensively with great success.

The leather that I have found most useful is the Niger goatskin, brought from Africa by the Royal Niger Company; it is a very beautiful colour and texture, and has stood all the tests tried, without serious deterioration. The difficulty with this leather is that, being a native production, it is somewhat carelessly prepared, and is much spoiled by flaws and stains on the surface, and many skins are quite worthless. It is to be hoped that before long some of the manufacturers interested will produce skins as good in quality and colour as the best Niger morocco, and with fewer flaws.

Much leather is ruined in order to obtain an absolutely even colour. A slight unevenness of colours is very pleasing, and should rather be encouraged than objected to. That the want of interest in absolutely flat colours has been felt is shown by the frequency with which the binders get rid of flat, even colours by sprinkling and marbling.

On this point I may quote from the committee: "The sprinkling of leather, either for the production of 'sprinkled' calf or 'tree' calf, with ferrous sulphate (green vitriol) must be most strongly condemned, as the iron combines with and destroys the tan in the leather, and free sulphuric acid is liberated, which is still more destructive. Iron acetate or lactate is somewhat less objectionable, but probably the same effects may be obtained with aniline colours without risk to the leather."

CHAPTER XX

Paper—Pastes—Glue

PAPER

Paper

PAPER may be made by hand or machinery, and either "laid" or "wove." "Laid" papers are distinguished by wire marks, which are absent in "wove" paper.

A sheet of hand-made paper has all round it a rough uneven edge called the "deckle," that is a necessary result of its method of manufacture. The early printers looked upon this ragged edge as a defect, and almost invariably trimmed most of it off before putting books into permanent bindings. Book-lovers quite rightly like to find traces of the "deckle" edge, as evidence that a volume has not been unduly reduced by the binder. But it has now become the fashion to admire the "deckle" for its own sake, and to leave books on hand-made paper absolutely untrimmed, with ragged edges that collect the dirt, are unsightly, and troublesome to turn over. So far has this craze gone, that machine-made paper is often put through an extra process to give it a sham deckle edge.

Roughly speaking, paper varies in quality according to the proportion of fibrous material, such as rag, used in the manufacture. To make paper satisfactorily by hand, a large proportion of such fibrous material is necessary, so that the fact that the paper is hand-made is to some extent a guarantee of its quality. There are various qualities of hand-made paper, made from different materials, chiefly linen and cotton rags. The best paper is made from pure linen rag, and poorer hand-made paper from cotton rag, while other qualities contain a mixture of the two or other substances.

It is possible to make a thoroughly good paper by machinery if good materials are used. Some excellent papers are made by machinery; but the enormous demand for paper, together with the fact that now almost any fibrous material can be made into paper, has resulted in the production, in recent years, of, perhaps, the worst papers that have ever been seen.

This would not matter if the use of the poor papers were restricted to newspapers and other ephemeral literature, but when, as is often the case, paper of very poor quality is used for books of permanent literary interest, the matter is serious enough.

Among the worst papers made are the heavily loaded "Art" papers that are prepared for the printing of half-toned process blocks. It is to be hoped that before long the paper makers will produce a paper that, while suitable for printing half-toned blocks, will be more serviceable, and will have a less unpleasant surface.

Several makers produce coloured hand-made papers suitable for end papers. Machine-made papers can be had in endless variety from any number of makers.

The paper known as "Japanese Vellum" is a very tough material, and will be found useful for repairing vellum books; the thinnest variety of it is very suitable for mending the backs of broken sections, or for strengthening weak places in paper.

The following delightful account of paper making by hand is quoted from "Evelyn's Diary, 1641–1706"—

"I went to see my Lord of St. Alban's house at Byflete, an old large building.

Thence to the paper mills, where I found them making a coarse white paper. They cull the raggs, which are linnen, for white paper, woollen for brown, then they stamp them in troughs to a papp with pestles or hammers like the powder-mills, then put it into a vessell of water, in which they dip a frame closely wyred with a wyre as small as a haire, and as close as a weaver's reede; on this they take up the papp, the superfluous water draining thro' the wyre; this they dextrously turning, shake out like a pancake on a smooth board between two pieces of flannell, then press it between a greate presse, the flannell sucking out the moisture; then taking it out they ply and dry it on strings, as they dry linnen in the laundry; then dip it in alum-water, lastly polish and make it up in quires. They put some gum in the water in which they macerate the raggs. The mark we find on the sheets is formed in the wyre."

Paper

The following are the more usual sizes of printing papers—

	Inches
Foolscap	17 × 13½
Crown	20 × 15
Post	19¼ × 15½

	Inches
Demy	22½ × 17½
Medium	24 × 19
Royal	25 × 20
Double Pott . . .	25 × 15
„ Foolscap .	27 × 17
Super Royal . . .	27 × 21
Double Crown . .	30 × 20
Imperial	30 × 22
Double Post . . .	31½ × 19½

The corresponding sizes of hand-made papers may differ slightly from the above.

Although the above are the principal named sizes, almost any size can be made to order.

The following is an extract from the report of the Committee of the Society of Arts on the deterioration of paper, published in 1898: "The committee find that the paper-making fibres may be ranged into four classes—

A. Cotton, flax, and hemp.
B. Wood, celluloses (*a*) sulphite process, and (*b*) soda and sulphate process.
C. Esparto and straw celluloses.
D. Mechanical wood pulp.

"In regard, therefore, to papers for books and documents of permanent value, the selection must be taken in this order, and always with due regard to the fulfilment of the conditions of normal treatment above dealt with as common to all papers.

"The committee have been desirous of bringing their investigations to a practical conclusion in specific terms, viz. by the suggestion of standards of quality. It is evident that in the majority of cases, there is little fault to find with the practical adjustments which rule the trade. They are, therefore, satisfied to limit their specific findings to the following, viz., *Normal standard of quality for book papers required for publications of permanent value.* For such papers they would specify as follows—

"*Fibres.* Not less than 70 per cent. of fibres of Class A.

"*Sizing.* Not more than 2 per cent. rosin, and finished with the normal acidity of pure alum.

"*Loading.* Not more than 10 per cent. total mineral matter (ash).

"With regard to written documents, it must be evident that the proper materials

Paper

are those of Class A, and that the paper should be pure, and sized with gelatine, and not with rosin. All imitations of high-class writing papers, which are, in fact, merely disguised printing papers, should be carefully avoided."

PASTES

Pastes

To make paste for covering books, &c., take $\frac{1}{4}$ lb. of flour, and $\frac{1}{2}$ oz. of powdered alum, and well mix with enough water to form a thin paste, taking care to break up any lumps. Add a pint of cold water, and heat gently in an enamelled saucepan. As it becomes warm, it should be stirred from time to time, and when it begins to boil it should be continually stirred for about five minutes. It should then form a thick paste that can be thinned with warm water. Of course any quantity can be made if the proportions are the same.

Paste for use is best kept in a wooden trough, called a "paste tub." The paste tub will need to be cleaned out from time to time, and all fragments of dry paste removed. This can easily be done if it is left, overnight, filled with water.

Before using, the paste should be well beaten up with a flat stick.

Pastes

For pasting paper, it should have about the consistency and smoothness of cream; for leather, it can be thicker. For very thick leather a little thin glue may be added. Paste made with alum will keep about a fortnight, but can be kept longer by the addition of corrosive sublimate in the proportion of one part of corrosive sublimate to a thousand parts of paste. Corrosive sublimate, being a deadly poison, will prevent the attack of bookworms or other insects, but for the same reason must only be used by responsible people, and paste in which it is used must be kept out of the way of domestic animals.

Several makes of excellent prepared paste can be bought in London. These pastes are as cheap as can be made, and keep good a long time.

Paste that has become sour should never be used, as there is danger that the products of its acid fermentation may injure the leather.

Paste tubs as sold often have an iron bar across them to wipe the brush on. This should be removed, and replaced by a piece of twisted cord. Paste brushes

Pastes

should be bound with string or zinc; copper or iron will stain the paste.

WHITE PASTE FOR MENDING

White Paste for Mending

A good paste for mending is made from a teaspoonful of ordinary flour, two teaspoonsful of cornflour, half a teaspoonful of alum, and three ounces of water. These should be carefully mixed, breaking up all lumps, and then should be heated in a clean saucepan, and stirred all the time with a wooden or bone spoon. The paste should boil for about five minutes, but not too fast, or it will burn and turn brown. Rice-flour or starch may be substituted for cornflour, and for very white paper the wheaten flour may be omitted. Ordinary paste is not nearly white enough for mending, and is apt to leave unsightly stains.

Cornflour paste may be used directly after it is made, and will keep good under ordinary circumstances for about a week. Directly it gets hard or goes watery, a new batch must be made.

Glue

It is important for bookbinders that the glue used should be of good quality, and the best hide glue will be found to answer well. To prepare it for use, the glue should be broken up into small pieces and left to soak overnight in water. In the morning it should be soft and greatly swollen, but not melted, and can then be put in the glue-pot and gently simmered until it is fluid. It is then ready for use. Glue loses in quality by being frequently heated, so that it is well not to make a great quantity at a time. The glue-pot should be thoroughly cleaned out before new glue is put into it, and the old glue sticking round the sides taken out.

Glue should be used hot and not too thick. If it is stringy and difficult to work, it can be broken up by rapidly twisting the brush in the glue-pot. For paper the glue should be very thin and well worked up with the brush before using.

The following is quoted from *Chambers's Encyclopædia* article on Glue—

Glue

"While England does not excel in the manufacture, it is a recognised fact that Scottish glue . . . ranks in the front of the glues of all countries. A light-coloured glue is not necessarily good, nor a dark-coloured glue necessarily bad. A bright, clear, claret colour is the natural colour of hide glue, which is the best and most economical.

"Light-coloured glues (as distinguished from gelatine) are made either from bones or sheepskins. The glue yielded by these materials cannot compare with the strength of that yielded by hides.

"A great quantity is now made in France and Germany from bones. It is got as a by-product in the manufacture of animal charcoal. Although beautiful to look at, it is found when used to be far inferior to Scottish hide glue."

PART II

CARE OF BOOKS WHEN BOUND

CHAPTER XXI

Injurious Influences to which Books are Subjected

Injurious Influences to which Books are Subjected

Gas Fumes.—The investigation of the Society of Arts Committee shows that—

"Of all the influences to which books are exposed in libraries, gas fumes—no doubt because of the sulphuric and sulphurous acid which they contain—are shown to be the most injurious."

The injurious effects of gas fumes on leather have been recognised for a long time, and gas is being, very generally, given up in libraries in consequence. If books must be kept where gas is used, they should not be put high up in the room, and great attention should be paid to ventilation. It is far better, where possible, to avoid the use of gas at all in libraries.

Light.—The committee also report that "light, and especially direct sunlight and hot air, are shown to possess deleterious influences which had scarcely been suspected previously, and the importance of moderate temperature and thorough ventilation of libraries cannot be too much insisted on."

The action of light on leather has a disintegrating effect, very plainly seen when books have stood for long periods on shelves placed at right angles to windows. At Oxford and Cambridge and at the British Museum Library the same thing was noticed. The leather on that side of the backs of books next to the light was absolutely rotten, crumbling to dust at the slightest friction, while at the side away from the light it was comparatively sound. Vellum bindings were even more affected than those of leather.

The committee advise that library windows exposed to the direct sunlight should be glazed with tinted glass.

Injurious Influences to which Books are Subjected

"Some attempts have been made to determine the effect of light transmitted through glasses of different colours, and they point to the fact that blue and violet glasses pass light of nearly as deleterious quality as white glass; while leathers under red, green and yellow glasses were almost completely protected. There can be no doubt that the use of pale yellow or olive-green glass in library windows exposed to direct sunlight is desirable. A large number of experiments have been made on the tinted 'cathedral' glasses of Messrs. Pilkington Bros., Limited, with the result that Nos. 812 and 712 afforded almost complete protection during two months' exposure to sunlight, while Nos. 704 and 804 may be recommended where only very pale shades are permissible. The glasses employed were subjected to careful spectroscopic examination, and to colour-measurement by the tintometer, but neither was found to give precise indications as to the protective power of the glasses, which is no doubt due to the absorption of the violet, and especially of the invisible ultra-violet rays. An easy method of comparing glasses is to expose under them to sunlight the ordinary sensitised albumenised photographic paper. Those glasses under which this is least darkened are also most protective to leather."

Tobacco.—Smoking was found to be injurious, and it is certainly a mistake to allow it in libraries.

"The effect of ammonia vapour, and tobacco fumes, of which ammonia is one of the active ingredients, was also examined. The effect of ammonia fumes was very marked, darkening every description of leather, and it is known that in extreme cases it causes a rapid form of decay. Tobacco smoke had a very similar darkening and deleterious effect (least marked in the case of sumach tanned leathers), and there can be no doubt that the deterioration of bindings in a library where smoking was permitted and the rooms much used, must have been partly due to this cause."

Damp.—Books kept in damp places will develop mildew, and both leather and paper will be ruined.

Where possible, naturally dry rooms should be used for libraries, and if not naturally dry, every means possible should be taken to render them so. It will sometimes be found that the only way to keep the walls of an old house dry is to put in a proper dampcourse. There are various other methods employed, such as lining the walls with thin lead, or painting them inside and out with some waterproofing preparation: but as long as a wall remains in itself damp, it is doubtful if any of these things will permanently keep the damp from penetrating.

Bookshelves should never be put against the wall, nor the books on the floor. There should always be space for air to circulate on all sides of the bookshelves. Damp is specially injurious if books are kept behind closely-fitting doors. The doors of bookcases should be left open from time to time on warm days.

Should mildew make its appearance, the books should be taken out, dried and aired, and the bookshelves thoroughly cleaned. The cause of the damp should be sought for, and measures taken to remedy it. Library windows should not be left open at night, nor during damp weather, but in warm fine weather the more ventilation there is, the better.

Heat.—While damp is very injurious to books on account of the development of mildew, unduly hot dry air is almost as bad, causing leather to dry up and lose its flexibility. On this point the Chairman of the Society of Arts Committee says:—

"Rooms in which books are kept should not be subject to extremes, whether of heat or cold, of moisture or dryness. It may be said that the better adapted a room is for human occupation, the better for the books it contains. Damp is, of course, most mischievous, but over-dryness induced by heated air, especially when the pipes are in close proximity to the bookcases, is also very injurious."

Dust.—Books should be taken from the shelves at least once a year, dusted and aired, and the bindings rubbed with a preservative.

To dust a book, it should be removed from the shelf, and without being opened, turned upside down and flicked with a feather duster. If a book with the dust on the top is held loosely in the hand, and dusted right way up, dust may fall between the leaves. Dusting should be done in warm, dry weather; and afterwards, the books may be stood on the table slightly open, to air, with their leaves loose. Before being returned to the shelves, the bindings should be lightly rubbed with some preservative preparation (see Chap. XXII). Any bindings that are broken, or any leaves that are loose, should be noted, and the books put on one side to be sent to the binder. It would be best when the library is large enough to warrant it, to employ a working bookbinder to do this work; such a man would be useful in many ways. He could stick on labels, repair bindings, and do many other odd jobs to keep the books in good repair.

Injurious Influences to which Books are Subjected

A bookbinder could be kept fully employed, binding and repairing the books of a comparatively small library under the direction of the librarian.

BOOKWORMS

Book-worms

The insects known as bookworms are the larvæ of several sorts of beetles, most commonly perhaps of *Anobium domesticum* and *Niptus hololeucus*. They are not in any way peculiar to books and will infest the wood of bookshelves, walls, or floors. A good deal can be done to keep "worms" away by using such substances

Book-
worms

as camphor or naphthalene in the bookcase. Bookworms do not attack modern books very much; probably they dislike the alum put in the paste and the millboards made of old tarred rope.

In old books, especially such as come from Italy, it is often found that the ravages of the bookworms are almost entirely confined to the glue on the backs of the books, and it generally seems that the glue and paste attract them. Probably if corrosive sublimate were put in the glue and paste used it would stop their attacks. Alum is said to be a preventive, but I have known bookworms to eat their way through leather pasted on with paste containing alum, when, in re-covering, the old wooden boards containing bookworms have been utilised in error.

When on shaking the boards of an old book dust flies out, or when little heaps of dust are found on the shelf on which an old book has been standing, it may be considered likely that there are bookworms present. It is easy to kill any that may be hatched, by putting the book in an air-tight box surrounded with cotton wool soaked in ether; but that will not kill the eggs, and the treatment must be repeated from time to time at intervals of a few weeks.

Book-worms

Any book that is found to contain bookworms should be isolated and at once treated. Tins may be put inside the boards to prevent the "worms" eating into the leaves.

Speaking of bookworms, Jules Cousin says—

"One of the simplest means to be employed (to get rid of bookworms) is to place behind the books, especially in the place where the insects show their presence most, pieces of linen soaked with essence of turpentine, camphor, or an infusion of tobacco, and to renew them when the smell goes off. A little fine pepper might also be scattered on the shelf, the penetrating smell of which would produce the same effect."

Possibly Keating's Insect Powder would answer as well as or better than pepper.

RATS AND MICE

Rats and Mice

Rats and mice will gnaw the backs of books to get at the glue, so means should be taken to get rid of these vermin if they should appear. Mice especially will

Rats and Mice

nibble vellum binding or the edges of vellum books that have become greasy with much handling.

COCKROACHES

Cock-roaches

Cockroaches are very troublesome in libraries, eating the bindings. Keating's Insect Powder will keep them away from books, but only so long as it is renewed at short intervals.

PLACING THE BOOKS IN THE SHELVES

Placing the Books in the Shelves

The Chairman of the Society of Arts Special Committee says on this point—

"It is important that a just medium should be observed between the close and loose disposition of books in the shelves. Tight packing causes the pulling off of the tops of book-backs, injurious friction between their sides, and undue pressure, which tends to force off their backs. But books should not stand loosely on the shelves. They require support and moderate lateral pressure, otherwise the leaves are apt to open and admit dust, damp, and mildew. The weight of the leaves also in good-sized volumes loosely placed will often be found to be resting on the shelf, making the backs concave, and spoiling the shape and cohesion of the books.

Placing the Books in the Shelves

"In libraries where classification is attempted there must be a certain number of partially filled shelves. The books in these should be kept in place by some such device as that in use in the British Museum, namely, a simple flat angle piece of galvanised iron, on the lower flange of which the end books rest, keeping it down, the upright flange keeping the books close and preventing them from spreading."

He also speaks of the danger to bindings of rough or badly painted bookshelves—

"Great care should be exercised when bookcases are painted or varnished that the surface should be left hard, smooth, and dry. Bindings, especially those of delicate texture, may be irreparably rubbed if brought in contact with rough or coarsely painted surfaces, while the paint itself, years after its original application, is liable to come off upon the books, leaving indelible marks. In such cases pasteboard guards against the ends of the shelves are the only remedy."

CHAPTER XXII

To Preserve Old Bindings—Re-backing

TO PRESERVE OLD BINDINGS

To Preserve Old Bindings

It is a well-known fact that the leather of bindings that are much handled lasts very much better than that on books which remain untouched on the shelves. There is little doubt that the reason for this is that the slight amount of grease the leather receives from the hands nourishes it and keeps it flexible. A coating of glaire or varnish is found to some extent to protect leather from adverse outside influences, but, unfortunately, both glaire and varnish tend rather to harden leather than to keep it flexible, and they fail just where failure is most serious, that is at the joints. In opening and shutting, any coat of glaire or varnish that has become hard will crack, and expose the leather of the joint and back. Flexibility is an essential quality in bookbinding leather, for as soon as the leather at the joint of a binding becomes stiff it breaks away when the boards are opened.

To Preserve Old Bindings

It would add immensely to the life of old leather bindings if librarians would have them treated, say once a year, with some preservative. The consequent expense would be saved many times over by the reduction of the cost of re-binding. Such a preservative must not stain, must not evaporate, must not become hard, and must not be sticky. Petroleum jelly has been recommended, and answers fairly well, but will evaporate, although slowly. I have found that a solution of paraffin wax in castor oil answers well. It is cheap and very simple to prepare. To prepare it, some castor oil is put into an earthenware jar, and about half its weight of paraffin wax shredded into it. On warming, the wax will melt, and the preparation is ready for use.

A little of the preparation is well worked into a piece of flannel, and the books rubbed with it, special attention being paid to the back and joints. They may be further rubbed with the hand, and finally gone over with a clean, soft cloth. Very little of the preparation need be used on each book.

If bindings have projecting metal corners or clasps that are likely to scratch the

To Preserve Old Bindings

neighbouring books, pieces of millboard, which may be lined with leather or good paper, should be placed next them, or they may have a cover made of a piece of millboard bent round as shown at fig. 120, and strengthened at the folds with linen. This may be slipped into the shelf with the book with the open end outwards, and will then hardly be seen.

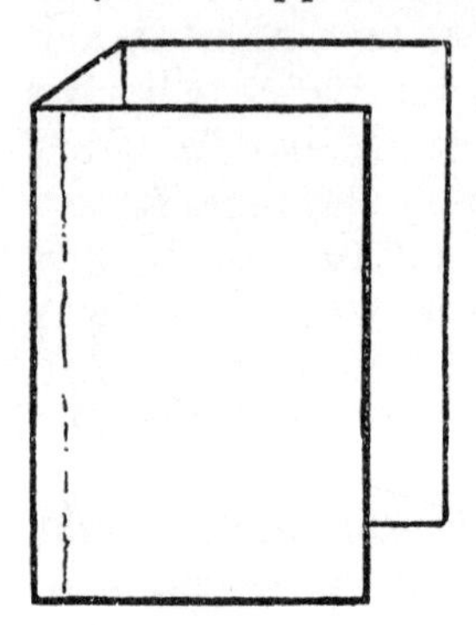

FIG. 120

Bindings which have previously had metal clasps, &c., often have projecting fragments of the old nails. These should be sought for and carefully removed or driven in, as they may seriously damage any bindings with which they come in contact.

To protect valuable old bindings, cases may be made and lettered on the back with the title of the book.

Loose covers that necessitate the bending back of the boards for their removal are not recommended.

Re-backing

Bindings that have broken joints may be re-backed. Any of the leather of the back that remains should be carefully removed and preserved. It is impossible to get some leathers off tight backs without destroying them, but with care and by the use of a thin folder, many backs can be saved. The leather on the boards is cut a little back from the joint with a slanting cut, that will leave a thin edge, and is then lifted up with a folder. New leather, of the same colour, is pasted on the back, and tucked in under the old leather on the board. The leather from the old back should have its edges pared and any lumps of glue or paper removed and be pasted on to the new leather and bound tightly with tape to make sure that it sticks.

When the leather at the corners of the board needs repairing, the corner is glued and tapped with a hammer to make it hard and square, and when it is dry a little piece of new leather is slipped under the old and the corner covered.

When the sewing cords or thread of a

Re-backing

book have perished it should be re-bound, but if there are any remains of the original binding they should be preserved and utilised. If the old boards have quite perished, new boards of the same nature and thickness should be got out and the old cover pasted over them. Such places as the old leather will not cover must first be covered with new of the same colour. Generally speaking, it is desirable that the characteristics of an old book should be preserved, and that the new work should be as little in evidence as possible. It is far more pleasant to see an old book in a patched contemporary binding, than smug and tidy in the most immaculate modern cover.

Part of the interest of any old book is its individual history, which can be gathered from the binding, book-plates, marginal notes, names of former owners, &c., and anything that tends to obliterate these signs is to be deplored.

SPECIFICATIONS

SPECIFICATIONS

These specifications will require modification in special

	I For Extra Binding suitable for Valuable Books. Whole Leather.	II For Good Binding for Books of Reference, Catalogues, etc., and other heavy Books that may have a great deal of use. Whole or Half Leather.
SHEETS.	To be carefully folded, or, if an old book, all damaged leaves to be carefully mended, the backs where damaged to be made sound. Single leaves to be guarded round the sections next them. All plates to be guarded. Guards to be sewn through. No pasting on or overcasting to be allowed.	As No. I, excepting that any mending may be done rather with a view to strength than extreme neatness.
END PAPERS.	To be sewn on. To be of good paper made with zigzag, with board papers of self-coloured paper of good quality, or vellum. Or to be made with leather joint.	To be of good paper made with zigzag, with board papers of self-coloured paper of good quality. Large or heavy books to have a cloth joint. To be sewn on.
PRESSING.	Books on handmade paper not to be pressed unduly.	Same as No. I.
EDGES.	To be trimmed and gilt before sewing. To be uncut.	To be cut, and gilt in boards or coloured, or to be uncut.
SEWING.	To be with ligature silk, flexible, round five bands of best sewing cord.	To be with unbleached thread, flexible, round five bands of best sewing cord.
BACK.	To be kept as flat as it can be without forcing it and without danger of its becoming concave in use.	Same as No. I.

cases, and are only intended to be a general guide.

III For Binding for Libraries, for Books in current use. Half Leather.	IV For Library Bindings of Books of little Interest or Value, Cloth or Half Linen.
Same as No. II.	Any leaves damaged at the back or plates to be overcast into sections.
To be of good paper, sewn on, made with zigzag.	Same as No. III.
Same as No. I.	
To be uncut, or to be cut in guillotine and gilt or coloured, or to have top edge only gilt.	May be cut smooth in guillotine.
To be with unbleached thread across not less than four unbleached linen tapes.	With unbleached thread over three unbleached linen tapes.
Same as for Nos. I and II.	Back to be left square after gluing up.

	I For Extra Binding suitable for Valuable Books. Whole Leather.	II For Good Binding for Books of Reference, Catalogues, &c., and other heavy Books that may have a great deal of use. Whole or Half Leather.
BOARDS.	To be of the best black millboard. Two boards to be made together for large books, and all five bands laced in through two holes.	Same as No. I, or may be of good grey board.
HEADBANDS.	To be worked with silk on strips of vellum or catgut or cord, with frequent tie-downs. The headbands to be "set" by pieces of good paper or leather glued at head and tail. The back to be lined up with leather all over if the book is large.	Same as No. I.
COVERS.	Goat-skin (morocco), pigskin or seal-skin manufactured according to the recommendations of the Society of Arts Committee on Leather for Bookbinding. Whole binding; leather to be attached directly to the back.	Same as No. I, excepting that properly prepared sheepskin may be added. Half-binding, leather only at back. Corners to be strengthened with tips of vellum. Sides covered with good paper or linen.
LETTERING.	To be legible and to identify the volume.	Same as No. I.
DECORATION.	To be as much or as little as the nature of the book warrants.	To be omitted, or only to consist of a few lines or dots or other quite simple ornament.
	All work to be done in the best manner.	Work may be a little rougher, but not careless or dirty.

III For Binding for Libraries, for Books in current use. Half Leather.	IV For Library Bindings of Books of little Interest or Value, Cloth or Half Linen.
To be split grey boards, or straw-board with black board liner, with ends of tapes attached to portion of waste sheet, inserted between them. Boards to be left a short distance from the joint to form a French joint.	To be split boards, two straw-boards made together and ends of slips inserted. French joint to be left.
To be worked with thread or vellum or cord, or to be omitted and a piece of cord inserted into the turn-in of the leather at head and tail in their place.	No headbands.
Same as Nos. I and II, but skins may be used where there are surface flaws that do not affect the strength. Leather to be used thicker than is usual, there being French joints. Leather at back only; paper sides; vellum tips.	Whole buckram or half linen and paper sides.
Same as Nos. I and II.	Same as Nos. I, II, and III.
To be omitted.	To be omitted.
Same as No. II.	Same as No. II.

APPENDIX

BY SYDNEY M. COCKERELL

ADHESIVES

Adhesives

CERTAIN of the polyvinyl adhesives can be used for a number of binding operations; for durability an internally plasticised PVA should be used. The spines of important books, however, should not be glued up with PVA adhesive as this can make it difficult to take the book down again without damaging the backs of the gatherings. For the repair of vellum leaves, use parchment size—a weak solution that just gells at room temperature. The size is made by cutting parchment into small pieces, soaking in water for several hours, boiling and straining. The size should be used warm, at about 40°C while it is still liquid. For the repair of paper leaves, a paste made from rice flour is less likely to stain than other adhesives. Rice flour 25 g, white Dextrin 5 g, water 265 ml.

ARMS BLOCKS

Arms Blocks

Arms blocks may be hand cut in brass or etched (binder's zinco). A brass block is easier to use but much more expensive than an etched block.

BOARD-CUTTER

Board-Cutter

A good board-cutter is a very valuable tool and most book-boards can be cut accurately on it, though a plough gives the best finished edge for thick boards. The cutter may also be used for trimming sections one at a time before sewing.

BOARD PAPERS

Board Papers

When pasting down the board paper the small pieces at the head and tail left from the cutting back of the end to show the turn in can be pasted and tucked in behind the joint of the book. This is neater and safer than sticking them to the edge of the board.

EDGE COLOURING

Edge Colouring

Spirit colours should be avoided as they are apt to run into the book.

EDGE GILDING

Edge Gilding

The edge should be set with a light burnish through paper about a quarter of an hour after the gold has been laid on, and burnished again through paper when the edge is dry, before giving the edge a light rub with beeswaxed leather and burnishing direct. Edge gilding is a tricky process which needs a great deal of practice to be sure about it; the quality of the paper, thickness of the glaire and the weather conditions have to be taken into account.

END PAPERS

End Papers

Inserting a free folded guard round the first and last section of the book before sewing is sound practice as it enables the fly leaf that is next to the book to open freely. I think this is one of the most useful contributions that I have made to binding.

FINISHING

Finishing

Note. Petrol should be used in place of benzene as benzene has been found to be very poisonous.

Misplaced tool impressions and dents on leather can sometimes be removed by damping the leather and repeatedly dabbing the place with a gluey finger and so lifting out the impression. This is less damaging than attempting to lift the leather with a pointed implement. Self-control must be exercised not to rub the place, as this will most certainly bruise and mark the leather. Pressure-adhesive tape pressed on and pulled off will sometimes remove small indentations.

Paste Wash. Paste washing is apt to show, particularly on dark leathers, and is seldom necessary for morocco though it is usually advisable to wash the cover up with diluted acetic acid (vinegar) before glairing. If the tooling should not stick it is often quicker and more satisfactory to wash the book up again with the dilute acetic acid and re-glaire, rather than re-glairing and mending in patches.

Brass Tools. The face of the tool may be engraved on ¼ in. thick brass sheet and the back of the face of the tool silver-soldered to the shank, as it is easier to engrave on a flat sheet than on the end of a shank. I have made, and had tools made in this way, and found them very satisfactory.

Designing for Tooling. Normally there are the colour of the leather and the three different textures of leather, gold tooling, and blind tooling to deal with. A free-hand sketch may be made and then interpreted with impressions of the tools through paper. A geometrical grid may be useful though its use does not necessarily mean that the pattern must be symmetrical in order to balance. The shape of the untooled spaces should be considered as well as the shape of the tooling, as these spaces or rests are very important. Lettering and units of tooling may be made out on separate pieces of paper so that the exact position can be arrived at by moving them about on a paper of the size of the book.

Binding design and decoration is based on tradition and grows from it; it is rightly influenced by the contemporary design of other objects. The present tendency is to use simple tools like stars and intersecting gold lines and gouges. Beginners must practise to gain technical skill but this is only a means to an end, and no amount of technical skill will make up for poor design. Therefore a binder who would develop a style of his own must think what he is doing and decide what it is he likes. This is a slow process and takes just as long as acquiring technical skill. It is hard work as it means thinking all the time and aiming at the final result of a well-designed binding suitable for its purpose with that little extra indefinable interest that is individual to the particular craftsman and can only be supplied by him, and it is this that makes handwork really worth while.

Fillets. One of 4 in. diameter will run more easily than one of a smaller diameter. I have made my own fillets fitted with ball races which makes them run very sweetly.

Handles. Asbestos finishing-tool handles have proved very satisfactory as they do not burn and therefore last very much longer than wooden handles and save the exasperation of loose tools.

Polishing Irons. If made of stainless steel they have the advantage of not rusting. The same applies to plating plates which are very much more durable when made of polished stainless steel than of nickel-plated iron.

Stoves. Electric finishing stoves are more pleasant to work over than gas-heated ones, but the tool ring must be properly designed so that the tools make good contact with the hot plate.

GLAIRE

Glaire

Some of the French shellac preparations work well; also the B.S. glaire evolved by W. Langwell.

GOLD LEAF

Gold Leaf

Single thickness, 1s. 6d. a book in 1901, 7s. 9d. a book in 1961. In 1972 only Italian gold leaf was available, at £1.04 per book. The prices given on page 202 are those of 1901.

LEATHER

Leather

The most durable material for binding is an alumed tawed skin, as this material is almost always in a strong condition, even on early bindings of the 12th century (unlike bindings in tanned skins, which are often in very poor condition). Vellum bindings, too, are generally in good condition, apart from occasional cockling. Although it is not usually possible for a bookbinder to check on the durability of leather, he can check on the strength of it—if the leather is weak and can be torn easily, it is not suitable for binding books.

LEATHER PARING

Leather Paring

A carpenter's steel spokeshave is an ideal tool for the paring of all but the edges of a cover. The spokeshave must be of the flat-sole type and should have two adjusting screws. The tool is intended for cutting wood but needs very little alteration to make it suitable for the paring of leather. With a new tool the corners of the blade should be rounded off on an oil stone and the cutting edge made slightly convex rather than concave. It must, of course, be very sharp. A small hand vice is convenient for holding the blade when sharpening. When in use the blade can be kept in good condition by drawing the spokeshave firmly along a leather strop. When paring, the leather is held in place by a G-clamp and a strip of wood, as both hands are needed for the spokeshave. Care must be taken not to mark the leather with the clamp.

LIBRARY BINDING

Library Binding

For many books it is better to sew on tapes and bind them with split boards and french joints as they will open more freely than they would if sewn on raised cords. There is a good deal to be said for a smooth spine as, besides being mechanically sound, it allows for greater freedom in decoration.

There is a great deal in favour of french joints as their use enables the leather to be thicker on this vulnerable point.

MARBLED PAPERS

Appendix

Marbled Papers

Marbled paper can be very useful for the ends and sides of books provided that the paper is strong and the pattern suitable. I started marbling paper for the fun of it and because we needed the paper for our books. We set out to make definite patterns and over a number of years we have learnt to control the process and found that the variations of pattern are almost unlimited. We have a basic handmade paper specially made for the purpose. Marbling, like edge gilding, is a tricky process with a large number of variable factors.

METAL WORK

Metal Work

The clasp as shown on fig. 119 should have a small rivet through it near the edge of the board to check the hook rising off the board. When metal work is to be used on a binding the boards should be of wood so that the metal may be securely attached by riveting through the boards and through a washer or plate that fits the rivet on the inside of the board. Tubular rivets with solid heads are satisfactory as they can be riveted with a ball punch on the inside of the board. Metal work that is held in place only by unclinched nails is liable to come adrift and to become scratchy and unpleasant. Silver nails that are used for decoration must be long enough to be clinched on the inside of the board. Silver will turn black in time unless it is plated with gold or rhodium: it is worth considering using oxidized metal and designing the binding to take the grey-black of oxidized silver. Metal work should be unobtrusive and smooth to handle without sharp corners.

PAPER

Paper

Machine-made paper has a grain and bends more freely with the grain than across it; therefore the grain should run vertically from head to tail of a book if the book is to open easily. When damped or pasted, paper swells or stretches very much more across the grain than the other way and correspondingly shrinks more across the grain. Therefore it is particularly important that the grain should run vertically from head to tail for end papers and also for hollow backs if they are to be put down without cockling. This also applies to machine-made board; the grain should run vertically, and when two cards are stuck together the grain should run the same way on both pieces and also the same way on any lining paper, as otherwise the board will be liable to twist. The amount of grain in paper depends on the speed of the paper-making machine.

Handmade paper and board do not have a grain and swell and shrink the same amount each way.

PAPER—ACIDITY

Paper—acidity

The acidity of paper is becoming an important factor in the conservation of books. It has been shown, particularly by W. Barrow in the U.S.A., that if paper is excessively acid it will deteriorate and finally disintegrate. The paper of many books is too acid and therefore needs deacidifying otherwise it will become hard and brittle. This deterioration will be more rapid in a high than in a low temperature. The acidity of paper may be checked with a pH meter or with a colour indicator. The scale is known as a pH scale. 7·0 is neutral, anything below is acid and anything above is alkaline. For durability paper should be between pH 6·0 and pH 8·0. Binders are beginning to take notice of this. In my bindery the paper of all books that come in for repair is checked with a pH meter and if necessary deacidified. Paper can be deacidified by immersion in a solution of calcium or magnesium bicarbonate. The bicarbonate has to be made before use by passing carbon dioxide through calcium or magnesium carbonate suspended in water.

PASTE

Paste

6 oz. flour; $\frac{1}{16}$ oz. thymol; 36 oz. water. Mix the flour to a smooth cream with a little of the water, add the full quantity of water, and allow to stand for one hour. Bring slowly to the boil, stirring continuously, and stop cooking as soon as it thickens. Cool to 120°F and stir in the thymol. The thymol must not be put in at a higher temperature as it will vaporise off.

SILK FOR SEWING

Silk for Sewing

This does not as a rule give sufficient swelling for a multi-section book. I think that a first-rate linen thread is preferable and is as durable as silk.

SINGLE-SECTION BOOKS

Single-section Books

These may be bound without split

boards by sticking the boards direct to the waste sheets. The end papers must be of good quality and there should be a sewn-in linen joint.

SIZING

Sizing

A water-jacketed size-bath that can be kept hot over a gas ring or by an electric immersion heater is safer than a directly-heated one. Photographic grade gelatine, 0·5-1·0 per cent, is satisfactory but papers vary, and the proportions may need to be adjusted for the particular book in hand. The strength of the sizing is affected by the amount of size squeezed out of the wet sheet in the press. The gelatine should be stirred into the hot water at 120°–140° F. When books have been thymolled the size should not be more than 120° F, as above this temperature the thymol will be vaporised and driven off from the books. A peel is a very useful tool for hanging wet sheets over drying lines; it can be made from a piece of wood 7 in. wide by 3 ft. long by ¼ in. thick with a 2 ft. 6 in. broom handle attached to the middle so as to form a T. The handle of the peel may be placed in a postal tube held by a finishing press on the floor so that the wet sheets may be hung over the cross-bar; the peel can then be lifted up and the sheets transferred to the drying lines.

STORING BOOKS

Storing Books

Proper ventilation is of the utmost importance for the safe storage of books. Book cases with doors should have a space between the shelf and the back of the case, or holes through the back of the shelves so that there may be a circulation of air.

Damp Books. When books have become damp by some accident of fire or other causes they should be kept in a cool place until they can be dealt with. They should not be piled up in a warm room with all the radiators turned on, as this will encourage the growth of mildew. The books may be fanned out and placed in a draught so that the air can dry them, or they may be interleaved with blotting paper provided the blotting paper is changed when it becomes damp. Stiff card at intervals in the book will help it to stand up.

Strong Rooms. If these are in the nature of dungeons with steel doors and no ventilation the books will most certainly become mildewed and moulder away, all the quicker if the unventilated strong room is heated, as heat without ventilation encourages the growth of mildew. The air of a strong room should be fresh like that of a good larder.

Appendix

THYMOLLING

Thymolling

When paper is mildewed it resists sizing just where the size is needed. Mildew can be killed and the paper left in a condition to absorb the size if it is passed through a solution of thymol in alcohol a the rate of 1 oz. of thymol to 64 oz. of spirit. Industrial spirit should be used, as methylated is liable to leave a stain on the paper. Another method of thymolling is to arrange the sheets in a closed cupboard with a tin lid of the thymol crystals over an electric bulb. The heat of the bulb causes the thymol to vaporise and fumigate the sheets.

TINS

Tins

Thin stainless steel Firth FMB No. 1 finish 23 SWG is much more serviceable than tinned iron sheet as it does not rust.

Tooling

A stylograph pen, such as a thick Rapidograph with the centre wire removed, can be very useful for glairing in lines and fine work. BS glaire can be kept in the pen, although the nozzle will need to be cleared with the wire before use, and the wire should be kept for this purpose.

VELLUM BINDINGS

Vellum Bindings

Vellum can be a very suitable binding material provided the construction of the book is suitable. Vellum has a hard surface and apparently it does not rot as some of the tanned leathers have done. For a vellum binding the book must have a hollow back and a wide french joint. The spine of the book should be lined with linen or leather under the hollow: linen for a small book and leather for a heavy one. Natural-toned vellum has more character than the white vellum and does not show marks and wear so readily as white vellum. Vellum can be used very satisfactorily for half bindings with cloth sides, or paper sides with vellum tips. There is a tendency for vellum-covered boards to warp outwards, particularly with sudden changes of humidity. This is sometimes noticeable in exhibitions where the binding may be exposed to an excessively dry atmosphere which will cause the boards to warp. This does not necessarily mean that the binding is at fault as the warping may be due to the outside of the boards becoming dry while the insides of the boards are relatively damp. The boards will probably go flat again when the book is returned to more normal conditions. The shape of the boards on a binding depends on the balance of pull between the covering material and the lining material. It is therefore important to let vellum bindings season for a week or more after covering so that extra lining papers may be added if necessary before putting down the end papers.

Whether the boards of a binding remain flat or not depends on the tension being the same on each side of the boards. If the boards of a vellum bound book are lined with vellum they are more likely to stay flat than when lined with some other material.

VELLUM BOOKS

Vellum Books

Vellum is an active material that swells and shrinks with changes of humidity.

Therefore adhesive must not be applied directly to the backs of vellum sections, as, besides the risk of the adhesive shrinking the vellum, there is the chance of cockling developing owing to the back of the leaves being held firmly by the adhesive while the rest of the leaf is free to swell or shrink with changes of atmosphere. Because of this it is a sound practice to fold a narrow guard of thin handmade paper round the back of each vellum section before sewing a book of vellum leaves, so that the adhesive will not come in contact with vellum. The adhesive sticks the guards together and enables the book to be shaped but leaves the vellum free to move. This method was developed through noticing that when old manuscripts had been glued up on the spine the glue was liable to break down between the sections, leaving an ugly gap when the book was opened; and in cases where the glue had held the book tended to be very stiff to open with horizontal cockles across the leaves.

VELLUM FINISHING

Vellum Finishing

Tooling on vellum is not as lasting as on leather as impressions on vellum tend to pull out in time. Nor is blind tooling satisfactory as the blind impressions do not change the colour of the vellum as they do on leather. Besides gold tooling vellum bindings can be lettered with Indian ink; it needs skill, and as a rule is a job for a scribe. In my bindery I employ a scribe for this purpose. The black lettering shows up very well in a library and very interesting results can be obtained with drawn black decoration combined with gold tooling.

VELLUM FLATTENING

Vellum Flattening

When vellum is made it is dried under tension. When it subsequently gets damp it cockles and tends to go back to the shape of the animal. To flatten it again it must be damped and dried under tension. Douglas Cockerell made some special apparatus for the flattening of the vellum leaves of the Codex Sinaiticus MS; the apparatus consisted of a strong wooden frame (like a picture frame) of about 2 ft. by 3 ft. 6 in. made of 2 in. by 1 in. section wood and mounted on four legs. Bulldog clips were lined with cloth and attached to one-pound lead weights by a length of cord. The clips were arranged round the edge of the vellum and the weight allowed to hang down over the edge of the frame so that the vellum was under tension. An alternative that is very much quicker to set up, is to place the Bulldog clips in position round the edge of the vellum leaf after it has been damped, and to pin the clips out on a soft wooden board by means of thick sewing needles fitted with wooden handles. For maps and documents that are written on one side only the vellum can often be damped direct on to the back with a sponge. Of course, great care must be taken to see that inks and colours do not run. Coloured initials must be treated very carefully indeed and gold initials must on no account be damped. If the colours are powdery and loose it may be advisable to paint over the colour with a thin solution of soluble nylon in I.M.S. (industrial methylated spirit).

GLOSSARY

Arming press, a small blocking press used for striking arms-blocks on the sides of books.

Backing boards, wedge-shaped bevelled boards used in backing (see Fig. 40).

Backing machine, used for backing cheap work in large quantities; it often crushes and damages the backs of the sections.

Band nippers, pincers with flat jaws, used for straightening the bands (see Fig. 61). For nipping up the leather after covering, they should be nickelled to prevent the iron staining the leather.

Bands, (1) the cords on which a book is sewn. (2) The ridges on the back caused by the bands showing through the leather.

Beating stone, the "stone" on which books were formerly beaten; now generally superseded by the rolling machine and standing press.

Blind tooling, the impression of finishing tools without gold.

Blocking press, a press used for impressing blocks such as those used in decorating cloth cases.

Board papers, the part of the end papers pasted on to the boards.

Bodkin, an awl, used for making the holes in the boards for the slips.

Bolt, folded edge of the sheets in an unopened book.

Cancels, leaves containing errors, which have to be

discarded and replaced by corrected sheets. Such leaves are marked by the printer with a star.

Catch-word, a word printed at the foot of one page indicating the first word of the page following, as a guide in collating.

Cutting boards, wedge-shaped boards somewhat like backing boards, but with the top edge square, used in cutting the edge of a book and in edge-gilding.

Cutting in boards, cutting the edges of a book after the boards are laced on.

Cutting press, when the lying press is turned, so that the side with the runners is uppermost, it is called a cutting press (see Fig. 46).

Diaper, a term applied to a small repeating all-over pattern. From woven material decorated in this way.

Doublure, the inside face of the boards, especially applied to them when lined with leather and decorated.

End papers, papers added at the beginning and end of a book by the binder.

Extra binding, a trade term for the best work.

Finishing, comprises lettering, tooling, and polishing, etc.

Finishing press, a small press used for holding books when they are being tooled (see Fig. 84).

Finishing stove, used for heating finishing tools.

Folder, a flat piece of ivory or bone, like a paper knife, used in folding sheets and in various other operations.

Foredge (fore edge), the front edge of the leaves. Pronounced "forrege."

Forwarding, comprises all the operations between sewing and finishing, excepting head-banding.

Gathering, collecting one sheet from each pile in a printer's warehouse to make up a volume.

Glaire, white of eggs beaten up, and used in finishing and edge gilding.

Groove, that part of the sections which is turned over in backing to receive the board.

Half binding, when the leather covers the back and only part of the sides, a book is said to be half bound.

Head and tail, the top and bottom of a book.

Headband, a fillet of silk or thread, worked at the head and tail of the back.

Head-cap, the fold of leather over the headband (see Fig. 67).

Imperfections, sheets rejected by the binder and returned to the printer to be replaced.

India proofs, strictly first proofs only of an illustration pulled on "India paper," but used indiscriminately for all illustrations printed on India paper.

Inset, the portion of a sheet cut off and inserted in folding certain sizes, such as duodecimo, &c. (see Fig. 4).

Inside margins, the border made by the turn-in of the leather on the inside face of the boards (see Fig. 116).

Joints, (1) the groove formed in backing to receive the ends of the millboards. (2) The part of the binding that bends when the boards are opened. (3) Strips of leather or cloth used to strengthen the end papers.

"*Kettle stitch*," catch stitch formed in sewing at the head and tail.

Lacing in, lacing the slips through holes in the boards to attach them.

Lying press, the term applied to the under side of the

cutting press used for backing, usually ungrammatically called "laying press."

Marbling, colouring the edges and end papers in various patterns, obtained by floating colours on a gum solution.

Millboard machine, machine used for squaring boards; should only be used for cheap work, as an edge cut by it will not be as square as if cut by the plough.

Mitring, (1) lines meeting at a right angle without overrunning are said to be mitred. (2) A join at 45° as in the leather on the inside of the boards.

Overcasting, over-sewing the back edges of single leaves or weak sections.

Peel, a thin board on a handle used for hanging up sheets for drying.

Plate, an illustration printed from a plate. Term often incorrectly applied to illustrations printed from woodcuts. Any full-page illustration printed on different paper to that of the book is usually called a "plate."

Pressing plates, plates of metal japanned or nickelled, used for giving finish to the leather on a book.

Press pin, an iron bar used for turning the screws of presses.

Proof, edges left uncut as "proof" that the book has not been unduly cut down.

Register, (1) when the print on one side of a leaf falls exactly over that on the other it is said to register. (2) Ribbon placed in a book as a marker.

Rolling machine, a machine in which the sheets of a book are subject to heavy pressure by being passed between rollers.

Sawing in, when grooves are made in the back with a saw to receive the bands.

Section, the folded sheet.

Semée or *Semis*, an heraldic term signifying sprinkled.

Set off, print is said to "set off" when part of the ink from a page comes off on an opposite page. This will happen if a book is pressed too soon after printing.

Sheet, the full size of the paper as printed, forming a section when folded.

Signature, the letter or figure placed on the first page of each sheet.

Slips, the ends of the sewing cord or tape that are attached to the boards.

Squares, the portion of the boards projecting beyond the edges of the book.

Start, when, after cutting, one or more sections of the book come forward, making the fore edge irregular, they are said to have started.

Straight-edge, a flat ruler.

Tacky, sticky.

T.E.G., top-edge gilt.

Trimmed. The edges of a book are said to be trimmed when the edges of the larger (or projecting) leaves only have been cut.

Tub, the stand which supports the lying press. Originally an actual tub to catch the shavings.

Uncut, a book is said to be uncut when the edges of the paper have not been cut with the plough or guillotine.

Unopened, the book is said to be unopened if the bolts of the sheets have not been cut.

Waterproof sheets, sheets of celluloid such as are used by photographers.

Whole binding, when the leather covers the back and sides of a volume, it is said to be whole bound.

Wire staples are used by certain machines in the place of thread for securing the sections.

REPRODUCTIONS OF BINDINGS

I, II, and III

Fifteenth Century Blind-tooled Bindings

IV

Sixteenth Century Binding with Simple Gold-tooling

V, VI, VII, and VIII

Bindings Designed by Douglas Cockerell

IX

Binding Designed by Douglas Cockerell, 1936

X

Binding Designed by Sydney M. Cockerell

XI and XII

Bindings Designed by Sydney M. Cockerell and Joan Rix Tebbutt

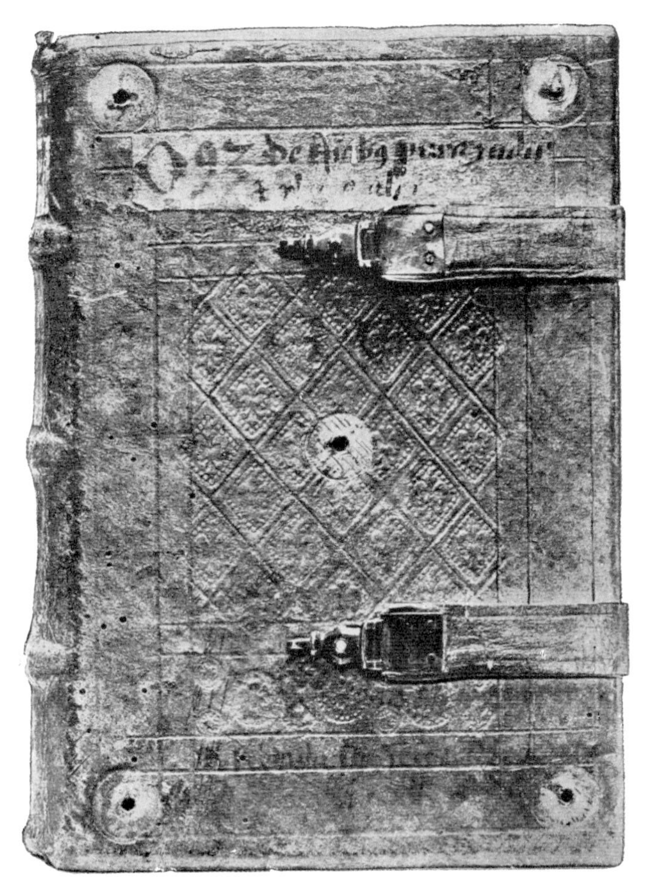

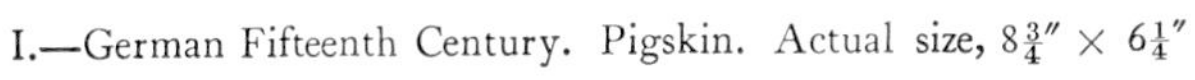

I.—German Fifteenth Century. Pigskin. Actual size, $8\frac{3}{4}'' \times 6\frac{1}{4}''$

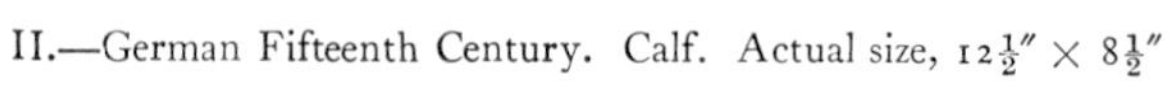

II.—German Fifteenth Century. Calf. Actual size, $12\frac{1}{2}'' \times 8\frac{1}{2}''$

III.—Italian Fifteenth Century. Sheepskin, with coloured roundels.
Actual size, $11\frac{1}{2}'' \times 8\frac{1}{4}''$

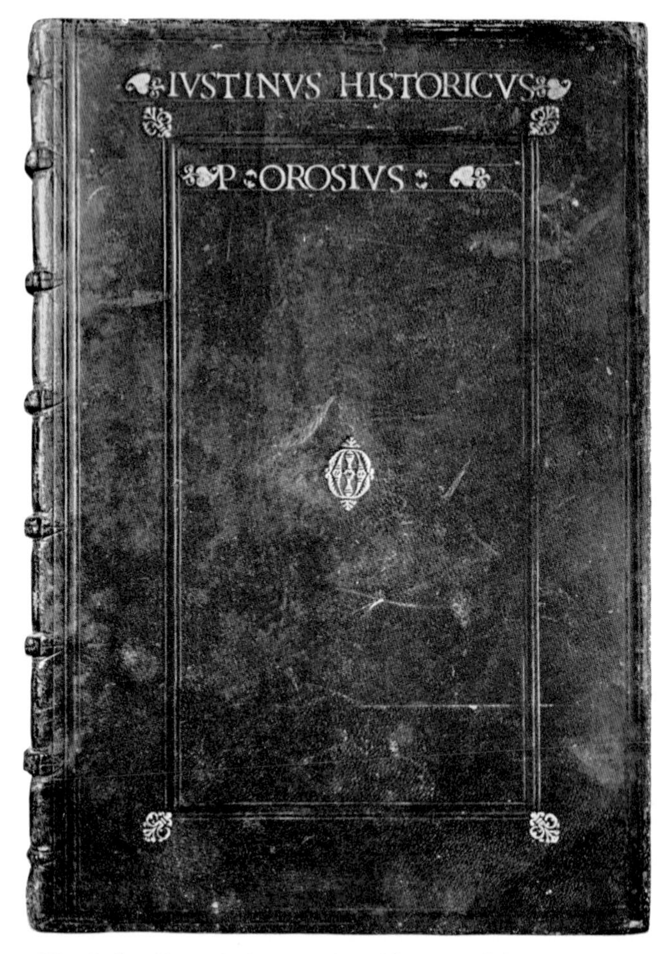

IV.—Italian Sixteenth Century. Goatskin. Actual size, $12\frac{1}{2}'' \times 8\frac{1}{2}''$

V.—Half Niger morocco, with sides of English oak.
Actual size, 17″ × 11½″

VI.—Niger morocco, onlaid leaves and shield
Actual size, $9\frac{3}{4}'' \times 6\frac{1}{2}''$

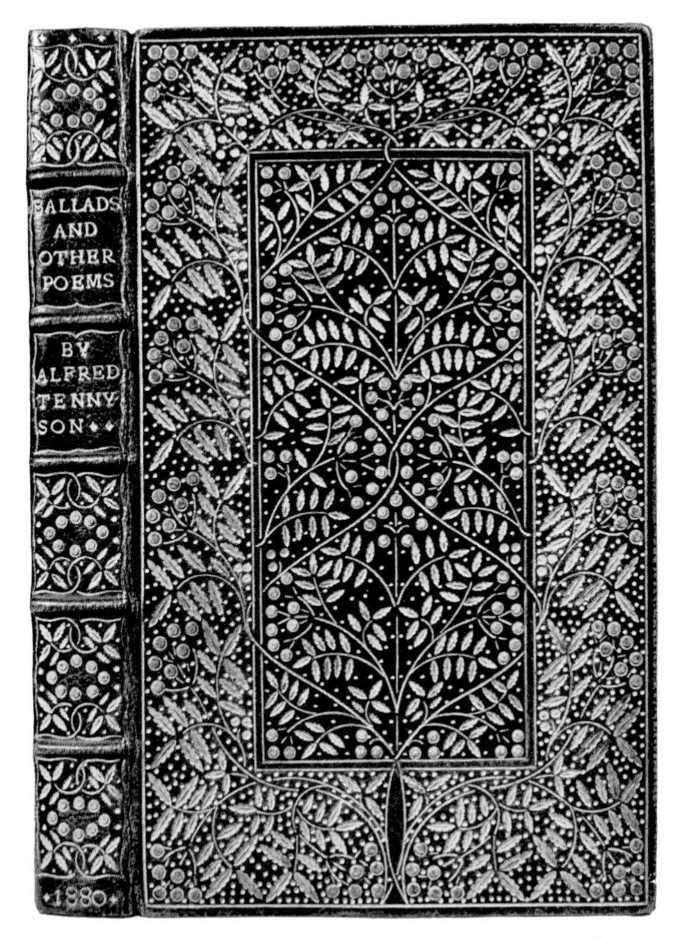

VII.—Green levant onlaid with lighter green panel and red dots.
Actual size, $6\frac{3}{4}'' \times 4\frac{1}{4}''$

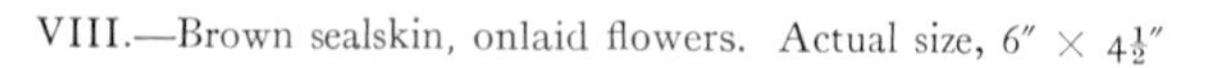

VIII.—Brown sealskin, onlaid flowers. Actual size, 6″ × 4½″

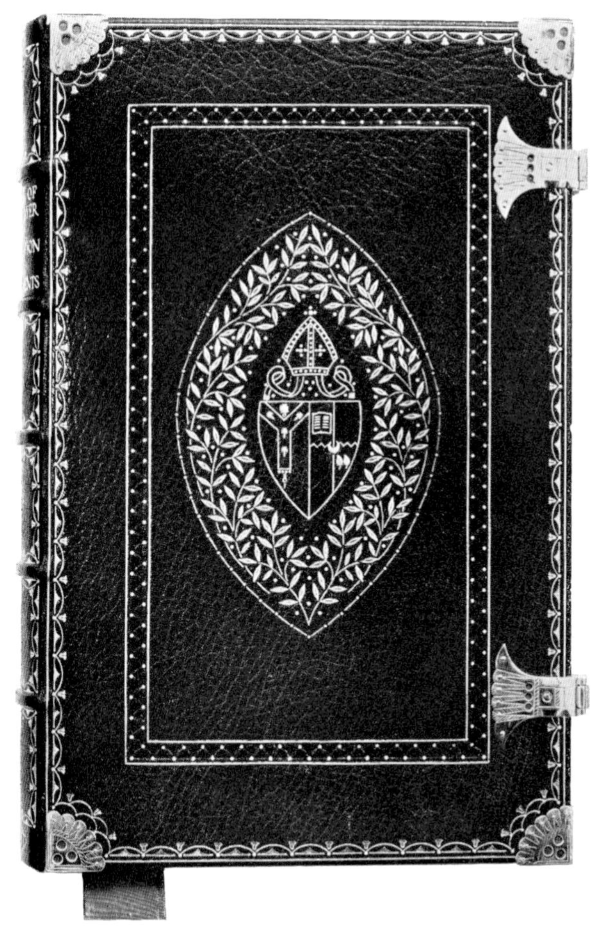

IX.—Prayer Book for Archbishop's Throne, Canterbury Cathedral. Grey blue levant morocco, gold and blind tooling, silver gilt clasps and corners with red inlay showing through them. Actual size, 15″ × 10″

(Reproduced by kind permission of the Friends of Canterbury Cathedral)

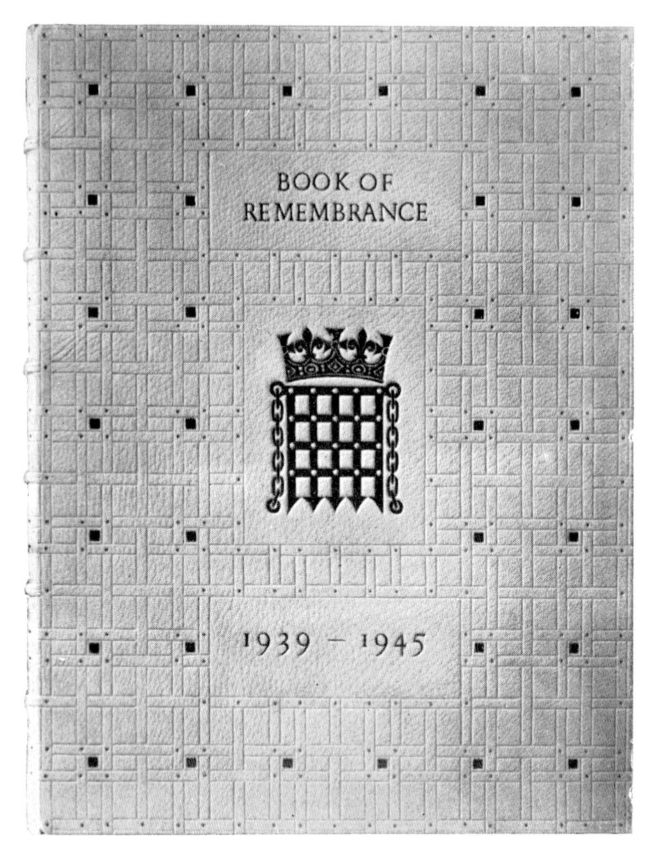

X.—House of Commons Book of Remembrance. White alumed morocco, gold and blind tooling. Actual size, 15″ × 11″

XI.—Incunabula, Aberdeen University Library. Vellum spines with black ink lettering

XII.—Lectern Bible for Chichester Cathedral. Dark blue morocco, silver gilt nails, gold tooling, oxidized silver clasps and shoes to the top and bottom edges of the boards. Actual size, 13″ × 10″

BIBLIOGRAPHY

Bibliography

The Craft of Bookbinding, Eric Burdett (David & Charles, London, 1975)

History of English Craft Bookbinding Technique, Bernard Middleton (Hafner Publishing Co., New York and London, 1963)

Introducing Bookbinding, Ivor Robinson (Batsford, London, 1968; Watson-Guptill, New York)

Modern Design in Bookbinding, Edgar Mansfield (Peter Owen, London, 1966; Boston Books, Boston)

Printing for Pleasure, John Ryder (Bodley Head, London, 1976)

Recommendations for Repair and Allied Processes for the Conservation of Documents BS 4971: Part 1: 1973 (British Standards Institution, 2 Park Street, London W1A 2BS)

The Repair of Books, Sydney Cockerell (Sheppard Press, London, 1958)

Restoration of Leather Bindings (American Library Associates, 1972)

Storage and Exhibition of Documents BS 5454:1977 (British Standards Institution, London)

Writing & Illuminating & Lettering, Edward Johnston (Pitman, London 1906; new ed. 1977 with Pentalic Corporation, New York)

INDEX

ADHESIVES, 313
Arming press, 229, 333
Arms blocks, 228, 314
Art paper, 48, 282
Autograph letters, 179

BACKING, 117
Backing hammer, 123
Back, lining up, 152
Band nippers, 160, 163
Bands, 333
Bandstick, 160
Beating, 90
Beating stone, 90, 333
Benzene, 315
Benzine, 207, 208, 209, 213
Binding, decoration of, 21, 30, 188, 233
Binding early printed books, 31, 46, 113
Binding, embroidered, 186
Binding, "extra," 308
Binding, jewelled, 263
Binding, library, 27, 173, 308
Binding manuscripts, 31, 108, 113, 125, 135, 223
Binding, metal-covered, 263
Binding, vellum, 180
Binding very thin books, 177, 323
Blind tooling, 188, 222
Blocking press, 229, 333
Blocks, striking, 229
Board papers, 314
Boards, 124
Boards, attaching, 132
Boards, cutting, 125, 314
Boards, filling in, 170
Boards, lining, 129
Boards, pressing, 193, 210
Boards, split, 28, 175, 311
Bodkin, 114
Bookbinding as a profession, 32
Books in sheets, 34
Bookworms, 297
Borders, 240, 253

CALF, 27, 277
Cancelled sheets, 43
Cased books, 19, 49
Castor oil, 303
Catch stitch, 99
Catch-words, 334
Celluloid, sheets of, 161
Centres, designing, 241
Chrome leather, 276
Clasps and ties, 183, 259
Cleaning off back, 137
Cloth casing, 19, 49
Cloth joints, 86, 257
Cobden-Sanderson, xii, 22
Cockroaches, 300
Coco-nut oil, 200
Collating, 43
Colouring edges, 144
Combining tools to form patterns, 232
Compasses, 131
Cord sewing, 111

Corners, mitring, 165, 168
Cousin, Jules, 74, 299
Covering, 23, 159, 176, 310
Crushing the grain of leather, 192
Cutting in boards, 139
Cutting millboards, 124
Cutting press, 128

DAMP, effect of, 294
Decoration of bindings, 21, 30, 188, 233, 317
Designing tools, 230
Diaper patterns, 236
Dividers, 51
Dots, striking, 205
Doublures, 253, 334
Dressing for old bindings, 302
Dust and dusting, 296

EARLY printed books, binding, 31, 46, 113
Edge colouring, 144, 314
Edge gauffering, 144
Edge gilding, 95, 144, 314
Edge sizing, 95, 146
Edges, painted, 146
Embroidered bindings, 186
End papers, 80, 254, 315
End papers, painted, 83
End papers, vellum, 84
Ends, silk, 84
Entering, 33
Evelyn's Diary, 282

FALSE bands, 26
Fillet, 190, 206, 246, 318
Filling in boards, 170
Finishing, 191, 315
Finishing press, 194
Finishing stove, 195, 318
Finishing tools, 188, 316
Flattening vellum, 65, 331
Folder, 164
Folding, 36
Fraying out slips, 114
French joint, 176
French paring knife, 156
French standing press, 91

GAS fumes, effect of, 291
Gathering, 35
Gauffering edges, 144
Gelatine, 70
Gilding edges, 95, 144
Gilt top, 92
Glaire, 97, 198, 318
Glass, tinted, for libraries 292
Glossary, 333
Glue, 289
Gluing up, 115
Goatskin, 277
Gold cushion, 200
Gold knife, 200
Gold leaf, 199, 319
Gold, net for, 96
Gold, pad for, 201
Gold tooling, 188, 191
Gouges, 189, 205, 245
Groove (*see* Joint)
Guarding, 42, 53
Guarding plates, 50, 56, 336

HAMMER, backing, 123
Hand-made paper, 280
Headbanding, 108, 147, 176
Head-caps, 156, 166
Heat, effect of, 295
Heraldry on bindings, 227
Hinging plates, 57
Hollow backs, 25, 185

IMPERFECTIONS, 35
India proofs, mounting, 63

India proofs, soaking off, 62
Indiarubber for gold, 207
Inlaying leather, 213, 232 243
Inlaying leaves or plates, 64
Inset, 40, 335
Inside margins, 253

JACONET, 60, 64
Japanese paper, 282
Japanese vellum, 282
Jewelled bindings, 263
Joint, 165, 169
Joint, cloth, 86, 257
Joint, French, 176
Joint, knocking out, 53
Joint, leather, 86, 171

KETTLE stitch, 49, 99, 105
Keys, sewing, 101
Knife, French paring, 156
Knife, gold, 200
Knife, mount cutters', 54
Knife, plough, 129, 139
Knocking down iron, 53, 134
Knocking out joints, 53
Knot, 100, 106

LACING in slips, 213
Lay cords, 100
Leather, 27, 263, 319
Leather, chrome, 276
Leather, crushing grain of, 192
Leather, inlaying, 213, 232, 243
Leather joints, 86, 171
Leather, paring, 154, 319
Leather, polishing, 191
Leather, sprinkling and marbling, 27, 279
Leather, stretching, 23, 161
Leather, testing, 274
Leather work, 226
Leaves, inlaying, 64
Lettering, 28, 215, 246
Letters, autograph, 179
Library binding, 27, 173, 308, 320
Light, effect of, on leather, 292
Lining up back, 152
Lithographic stone, 157, 160
Loose covers, 304
Lying press, 128

MANUSCRIPTS, binding, 31 108, 113, 125, 135, 223
Manuscripts, collating, 46
Maps, throwing out, 60
Marbled paper, 83, 321
Margins, inside, 253
Marking up, 98
Materials for sewing, 111
Mending, 76
Mending tooling, 208
Mending vellum, 79
Metal on bindings, 262, 321
Millboard machine, 127, 313, 336
Millboard shears, 126
Millboards, 124
Mitring corners, 165, 168
Morocco, 277
Morocco, "Persian," 271
Mount cutters' knife, 54
Mounting India proofs, 63
Mounting very thin paper, 63

NET for gilding edges, 96
Niger morocco, 278
Nippers, band, 160, 163
Nipping press, 211

OIL, coco-nut, 200
Opening books, 257
Overcasting, 51
"Overs," 35
Oxalic acid, use of, 173

PAD for gold, 201
Paging, 44
Painted edges, 146
Painted end papers, 83
Pallets, 189
Paper, 280, 322-4
Paper, art, 48, 283
Paper, hand-made, 280
Paper, Japanese, 282
Paper, marbled, 83
Paper, sizes of, 36, 283
Paper, sizing, 67
Paper, splitting, 63
Paper, washing, 71
Paraffin wax, 303
Paring leather, 154
Paring paper, 61
Paring stone, 157, 160
Paste water, 198
Pastes, 286, 324
Pasting down end papers, 254
Patterns, 232
"Peel," 325, 336
Permanent binding, 19
"Persian" morocco, 271
Pigskin, 278
Plates, detaching, 48
Plates, guarding, 56
Plates, hinging, 57
Plates, inlaying, 64
Plates, trimming, 40
Plough, 128
Plough knife, 129, 139
Polishing, 191, 318
Preserving old bindings, 302
Press, arming, 229, 333
Press, blocking, 229, 333
Press, cutting, 128
Press, finishing, 194
Press, lying, 128
Press, nipping, 211
Press pin, 336
Press, sewing (*see* Sewing frame)
Press, standing, 88
Pressing boards, 193, 210
Pressing in boards, 138
Pressing plates, 192, 336
Pressing sections, 87
"Proof," 336
Publishers' binding, 20
Pulling to pieces, 46

QUARTER sections, 42
Quires, books in, 34

RATS and mice, 299
Re-backing, 305
Re-binding, 18, 306
Re-folding, 51
Register of printing, 52, 336
Representations of bindings, plates I-XII
Roll, 190
Rounding, 117

SAWING in, 20, 25, 100, 108
Scrap-books, 178
Sealskin, 278
Sections, pressing, 87
Sewing, 100
Sewing cord, 111
Sewing frame, 100
Sewing keys, 101
Sewing on tapes, 26, 111, 174

Sewing on vellum slips, 111, 181
Sewing silk, 112
Sewing, tape for, 112
Sewing thread, 112
Sheepskin, 277, 310
Sheets, books in, 34
Sheets, waterproof, 161
Signatures, 34, 43
Silk ends, 84
Silk sewing, 112, 324
Sizes of paper, 36, 283
Sizing, 67, 325
Sizing edges, 95, 146
Sizing leather, 198
Sizing paper, 67
Slips, 337
Slips, fraying out, 114
Slips, lacing in, 132
Soaking off India proofs, 62
Society of Arts, Reports of Committees, 22, 264, 284
Specifications, 308
Split boards, 28, 175, 311
Splitting paper, 63
Sprinkling leather, 27, 279
Squares, 131, 153, 337
Standing press, 88
Standing press, French, 89, 91
Staples, wire, 49
"Starred" sheets, 43
Stone, lithographic, 157, 160
Storing books, 326
Stove, finishing, 195, 318
Striking dots, 205
Striking tools, 204

TAPE, sewing on, 26, 112, 174
Temporary binding, 20
Testing leather, 274
Thin books, binding, 177
Thin paper, mounting, 63
Thread, sewing, 112
Throwing out maps, 60
Thymolling, 327
Ties and clasps, 183, 259
Tobacco smoke, effect of, on binding, 294
Tooling, 328
Tooling, blind, 188, 222
Tooling, gold, 24, 188, 191
Tooling on vellum, 212
Tools, designing, 188, 230
Tools, finishing, 188, 230
Training for bookbinding, 32
Trimming before sewing, 93
Trimming machine, 94
Trimming plates, 40
Tub, 337
Tying up, 167

VARNISH, 209
Vellum binders, 26
Vellum bindings, 180, 328
Vellum books, 329
Vellum ends, 84
Vellum, flattening, 65, 331
Vellum, Japanese, 282
Vellum, mending, 79
Vellum slips, sewing on, 111, 183
Vellum, tooling on, 212, 330

WALKER, Emery, 216
Washing, 71
Waterproof sheets, 161
Weaver's knot, 106
Wooden boards, 32, 135, 223
Worm holes, 78, 297